When All Else Fails

Some New and Old Tools for Doing Brief Therapy

Rubin Battino, MS

Crown House Publishing Limited
www.crownhouse.co.uk
www.crownhousepublishing.com

First published by

Crown House Publishing Ltd
Crown Buildings, Bancyfelin, Carmarthen, Wales, SA33 5ND, UK
www.crownhouse.co.uk

and

Crown House Publishing Company LLC
6 Trowbridge Drive, Suite 5, Bethel, CT 06801, USA
www.crownhousepublishing.com

First Published 2015.

BRITISH LIBRARY OF CATALOGUING-IN-PUBLICATION DATA
A catalogue entry for this book is available from the British Library.

Print ISBN 9781845908942
Mobi ISBN 9781845909420
ePub ISBN 9781845909437

LCCN 2014954327

Printed in the U.S.A.

Contents

Preface

Since Chapter 1 gives an introduction to this book in terms of how I got to write it, and its contents (among other things), I am going to use this space for acknowledgments.

Howard H. Fink, Ph.D., was initially my therapist, then my trainer in Gestalt Therapy, and later a colleague and friend. I have learned much from him over the years, both about being a therapist and about life. Between 2000 and 2007 I recorded many conversations in his office. These were transcribed, and I converted the conversations into a book (Fink and Battino, 2011). You may find "eavesdropping" on our conversations to be interesting.

My colleague Joe Emanuel of the Counseling Department at Wright State University was a friend, and my mentor and research advisor for my master's degree in counseling. I took several courses from Joe and always marveled at the way he "bounced" into the classroom full of energy and vitality and good humor. He was a remarkable teacher.

Although I never met Milton H. Erickson, M.D., I felt that I knew him, since for a period of time I was so immersed in his writings and tapes and movies that I could sense his presence. This was particularly the case when I was writing a play about his life (Battino, 2008). I learned much from him in this way, and also much from people he taught, such as Ernest L. Rossi, Jeffrey K. Zeig, Kay F. Thompson, and David B. Cheek.

I did meet Viktor Frankl several times in Vienna. In many ways I got to know him better when I was researching the biography I wrote about him in play form (Battino, 2002). His messages of hope and finding meaning in life have influenced millions, and they certainly impacted my life.

For the shape of this book I owe much to the careful readings of it by my friend and colleague Michael F. Hoyt, Ph.D. His suggestions for revisions were many and were taken to heart. Thank you, Michael.

I sometimes joke that I write so much because otherwise my wife Charlotte would find things for me to dust! (This not true, since she knows that I can "dust" the entire house in under two minutes!) We have been married for over fifty-four years and we still find interesting things to talk about, and wonderful places to visit together. Charlotte has a strong sense of reality, and can certainly put whatever I do into perspective. We marvel that somehow our two sons, David and Benjamin, have turned out to be such fine human beings. We also marvel further that their respective wives, Hazuki and Jill, are the same. David and Hazuki's two sons, Toma and Miaki, are great people. And, Benjamin and Jill's six children—Ellie, Lily, Anabel, Asa, Abel, and "Little" Ben—are all grandchildren to be proud of.

As you will read later, what is really, really, really important in life are my relationships with all of those mentioned above, my blood relatives, my extended family, and Nature.

—Rubin Battino

Foreword

Michael F. Hoyt, Ph.D.

I first heard Rubin Battino teach a brief therapy workshop, then met him through several of his books—*Metaphoria, Expectation, Ericksonian Approaches,* and *Healing Language.* We became acquainted as colleagues at conferences, and more recently, I have had the pleasure of spending friendly time with him and his lovely wife, including a long lunch and a walk through our local Marin County national monument, the beautiful Muir Woods. It is thus with multilayered pleasure that I welcome his latest book, *When All Else Fails: Some New and Some Old Tools for Doing Brief Therapy,* which, dear reader, you hold in hand.

All that is new is not true, and all that is true is not new. There is much in this fine volume to commend it, including reviews on hypnosis and ideomotor signaling, NLP, bioenergetics, psychodrama, Gestalt Therapy, and other approaches that are often overlooked today. What I like the most, however, is the emphasis on what is too frequently given quick lip service in much current therapy training: the importance of the alliance, the role of expectations, and the conscious and skillful use of language. There is plenty of useful technical information here—some from older approaches, some *au courant*—but what matters most is the human relationship. Clients don't care what you know until they know that you care, and the therapeutic alliance is the soil in which therapy techniques may (or may not) take root. Please, take heed.

Rubin is a seasoned and wise clinician. He provides a thoughtful, personal guide that can enhance the effectiveness of your work with clients, regardless of your theoretical orientation. There are lots of ideas and methods in this fine book that will be of interest. I enjoyed it, and expect that you will too!

—Mill Valley, CA

Part I

Ideas, Approaches, and Concerns

Chapter One

Introduction

1.1 How This Began

For a number of years now I have been doing workshops of various lengths on topics such as an introduction to hypnosis, very brief therapy, and guided imagery. The attendees have been relatively young, mostly under forty, with a significant number still in graduate school. My style of presentation involves an outline of the workshop which is generally completely covered, and random thoughts about related subjects that pop into my head as I go along. I also tell stories. From time to time my thoughts stray from the regular material to discussing other forms of therapy than the one I am presenting. The "very brief therapy" workshop does include discussions of many methods and approaches. What I have invariably found is that a large proportion of those attending have never heard of many of the things I talk about. Of course, lots of approaches have gone "out of fashion," so to speak. Yet, I believe it is important for modern day therapists to know about how therapy has changed and developed over time. Is psychodrama an anachronism or even, perhaps, an artifact? How many therapists know about Gestalt Therapy and use it in their practice? Cognitive Behavioral Therapy (CBT) seems to have won out over many other approaches since it has the blessing of presumably being "evidence-based." It is almost as if the experiential evidence of effectiveness of those who have studied and participated in psychodrama, for example, no longer counts!

At the present time counselors, social workers, and psychologists do face-to-face talk therapy. Psychiatrists appear to be stuck in the medical model wherein finding the right drug to match a particular diagnosis is the norm. For them, with less than ten minutes face time with each patient talk therapy is not possible, and is just a thing from the past. Michael D. Yapko is a recognized international authority on chronic depression. He uses hypnosis in ten to twelve sessions for chronic depression, and in his experience this results in "cures" in the sense that his clients are no longer chronically depressed. The medical model approach has clients on anti-depressive drugs forever, or seemingly forever. Hypnosis has no side effects. The drugs usually take one or two months to have an effect. Also, anti-depressive drugs are typically changed and adjusted in dosage over the time the patient sees a psychiatrist. That is, finding the right drug and dosage for a particular patient appears to be almost a hit-and-miss approach. Yet I suspect that these drugs (and other psychotropic medicines) are popular, since all the patient has to do is pop a pill, rather than visit a talk therapist over a period of several months. Initially, popping pills appears easier, even if it is not more effective!

Please note that I am not against medication when used appropriately in some time-limited fashion (or long term if needed). Medications certainly appear to help many people on a short term basis, and are frequently useful in emergency situations. The medical model works for medical difficulties. For mental health concerns talk therapy is still the best bet as far as I am concerned. I could cite difficulties with the usefulness and accuracy of the Diagnostic and Statistical Manual, 2013 (DSM), but have already done so in an earlier book (Battino, 2006). In that book I also cited studies on the effectiveness of using psychoactive drugs. Double-blind studies on those drugs always show that placebos have a high degree of effectiveness. To my mind, unless a drug is *significantly* better than a placebo it is questionable as to whether it should be prescribed. After all, placebos have no side effects! As a last comment here it should be noted that in many of these double-blind studies the test subjects were able to distinguish between whether they were taking placebos or the test drug. One outcome of these studies is that it is now sometimes the case that placebos are adjusted to give some discernible side effects!

My friend and colleague Luciano L'Abate has published a great deal (see Chapter 9) about the demise of face-to-face (f2f) talk therapy, and its being replaced by distance learning and workbooks. We disagree about this, and my main argument is that the approach he is proposing invariably includes some f2f sessions. A person can download workbooks on particular areas (such as depression) on-line, and then carry out the instructions. Writing about one's personal difficulties has long been a useful modality; workbooks and medications and f2f all have a place in helping people in distress. A principle of cybernetics (requisite variety) states, "In any complex system, the component with the most variability controls." For the two-person interaction between a therapist and a client to be effective the therapist must have more variability in the interaction than the client. That is, in the immediacy of the interaction the therapist needs to have many choices of response at their disposal, and be flexible in this. A therapist who only knows CBT, for example, is at a disadvantage.

1.2 Rapport Building

The so-called "therapeutic alliance" has been well studied (Wampold, 2001). What is meant by therapeutic alliance is that there is something in the way the therapist and client interact that gives the client the feeling that the therapist is on their side—a companion, friend, ally, helper—working through the client's concerns to outcomes that the client wants. This ally is with them in their struggle to becoming comfortable with themselves, and in becoming capable of taking care of themselves. That is, the client is not isolated or alone with a technician who provides some sort of mechanical or verbal fix.

In the old days of psychotherapy the therapist was endowed with almost magical powers to help/fix the client. The therapist knew best and was the "operator" while the client was the "subject." (This aura of operator/subject still exists in many medical interactions where the medical doctor is imbued with esoteric special knowledge and skills. This is realistic in many ways, and I certainly trusted the knowledge and skills of my orthopedic surgeon and his staff when he gave me an artificial knee several years ago.) When working with mental health concerns, in addition to being knowledgeable and skillful, the therapist also has to be a real person in her interactions with a client. Within the isolated four walls of a consulting room two individuals meet, and the therapist is privileged to share in the life and world of the client. That meeting of two human beings can be enhanced by the knowledge, practice and skill of rapport building.

In almost all of my books relating to psychotherapy there is a chapter on rapport building. This was done deliberately as it is always important for you and your client to fit into the world in similar ways, i.e. your personal and human connection. It is done deliberately here because in my workshops I have discovered that many of the attendees have been "exposed" to this in their training, but not to the depth and degree that is needed in my judgment. So, in this section I am going to go over the basics of establishing rapport once again.

My colleague, Thomas L. South, Ph.D., believes the essence of establishing rapport is in *pacing and leading*. That is, when you are in rapport with someone you are pacing their five-dimensional existence in the world in some way. In addition to the XYZ coordinates of space there are time and the emotional/physical or mind/body coordinate or parameter. Once you have paced them, then you can lead them into useful ideas and feelings.

There are two basic ways of establishing rapport: verbal and postural. In *verbal pacing* you match your client's speech patterns in some manner. We all have unique ways of speaking. Some characteristics of speech are: speed, tempo, accent, rhythm, and loudness or softness. If your client speaks rapidly, you increase your rate of speech just enough for them to know that you are speaking faster. You need to match only *one* of the patterns of speech for them to have a sense that you are speaking in the same manner. If a client has a regional speech pattern (like from the South or West or Bostonian), you need to *subtly* match their speech. If you mimic them exactly, they will know that you are doing this. So, with a Southerner you can add some musicality or rhythm to your speech without going overboard. The pacing has to effectively be subliminal to work. Practice this by sub-vocalizing when in the presence of others.

People tend to describe the world they live in using primarily visual, auditory, or kinesthetic (physical) words. In the field of Neurolinguistic Programming (NLP) this is called *representational systems*. That is, people see things clearly, hear them soundly, or feel them physically. Listen for how people describe the world around them, and talk back to them in their preferred representational system. There are also neutral words that are not in one of these systems, like sense, believe, and process. Since the meaning of any communication is the response that you get and not your intent, you need to be sensitive to how your clients react and respond to what you say. Pay attention to them and not your own internal states. Intuition may be fed by awareness, but close observation is safer. When in doubt, ask. Also, practice using all three representational systems in your communication.

Everyone has preferred ways of fitting three-dimensionally into the world. Most of this is learned in childhood by children mimicking parents in how they sit, stand, and walk. Does your client lean toward you or away from you or sit upright? Do they make eye contact or avoid it? Are their legs or arms crossed or not? How does their posture change during a session? Do they walk stiffly or smoothly? Do they fidget or sit quietly? Postures need to be paced subtly, and you only need to pace *one* physical attribute to establish rapport. In his early days Milton H. Erickson actually followed people and imitated their way of walking so that he could literally "walk in their footsteps." I heard Leslie Cameron Bandler on a tape describe how she paced and led a depressed client out of depression by first matching a soft voice delivered from a hunched over position and slowly increasing her own volume as she slowly straightened up. This kind of pacing and leading (postural pacing) needs to occur out of the client's conscious awareness—subtly.

Perhaps the most important physical characteristic to pace is the rate and depth of breathing. The way we breathe is generally outside of conscious awareness, and yet is essentially organic and primal/primitive. Pace your speech to your client's breathing rate. (This is especially important when you are doing hypnotic work or any work involving the client going "inside" of himself.) Once breathing is paced you can *lead* to slower or faster rates as the situation requires. Breathing rates can be detected by observing shoulder and clothing movements (but do not stare at someone's chest!). Pacing breathing can be practiced in any social setting, and can be done unobtrusively from behind people by looking at their shoulders.

1.3 Therapeutic Alliance

Therapy is best done as a collaborative effort where you are the *guide* and not the director. For this it is useful to believe that everyone has within them the resources needed to bring about the changes in their lives that they desire. You need to find out in the initial interview what it is that they want out of meeting with you so that you and they both know if the work you do together has been successful. A goal of "feeling better" needs to be spelled out in operational and behavioral terms. What will have changed in their lives once they feel better? Are the goals realistically attainable? Much careful listening is required.

Clients come to you because they are stuck in behaviors and emotions that they have been unsuccessful in getting out of on their own. Initially, you need to know what they have tried that has *not* worked, for it is fruitless to repeat unsuccessful attempts. In this regard the Brief Family Therapy Center of Milwaukee's three rules apply:

1. If it is not broken, don't fix it.
2. If it worked once, do it again.
3. If it doesn't work, don't do it again. Do something different.

Being stuck means that in effect they have *one* interpretation of events in their life, and that this interpretation has resulted in *one* response. Collaboratively, you then need to discover other relevant and realistic interpretations and responses. That is, the outcome is a *variety of choices*. In essence, this is changing the client's "I can't" to "I won't" or what they perceive as involuntary behavior to voluntary behavior. Reframing (see Chapter 23) is an excellent way of providing choice.

The therapeutic alliance involves a conversation between two people. Since you have been down this road before, during the conversation you can provide some guidance as to choices based on your own personal experiences and knowledge. In this role you are more like a wise mentor or relative than an authoritarian figure. However, this is not to ignore that there are times when it is important to be directive. Although Milton Erickson was mainly known for indirection via the use of metaphors and stories, he was also forcefully directive when appropriate.

1.4 Overview of Parts I and II

Part I is composed mainly of presentations of various topics, and Part II describes in some detail a number of alternative approaches that continue to have much effectiveness in helping clients change and become comfortable in their lives. So you know what to expect, I will briefly describe each chapter. The alternative and older approaches discussed in Part II are actually some of the most frequent things I do with clients, and many of them are sadly no longer taught or practiced.

Chapter 2. *Expectation: The Essence of Brief Therapy*—Expectation is the essence of the placebo effect and sets the person up for rapid change. Single-session therapy, the placebo and related effects are discussed.

Chapter 3. *The Power of Pauses in Hypnosis and Psychotherapy*—Novice therapists typically talk too much and tend to fill up space with their own voice. A client needs to have time to process and digest and think about what is going on. This is especially important in hypnosis sessions.

Chapter 4. *Poetry in Hypnosis and Psychotherapy*—Poetic language stretches the imagination of the listener in beautiful and thoughtful ways, and it is the imagination which needs to be stirred for effective change to occur.

Chapter 5. *Dreams, Hopes, and Unfulfilled Desires*—Without the internal driving force of dreams, hopes and unfulfilled desires, what is there to give meaning in life?

Chapter 6. *Chatting as Therapy*—When you are a professional healer (one who is paid) you are generally endowed by your clients with special powers, knowledge, and abilities. In effective psychotherapy this needs to be moderated by being human; a real and fallible person who is sharing an important portion of the client's life. I call this "chatting."

Chapter 7. *On the Importance of Healing Language*—Language can be harmful, helpful, or healing—you must be sensitive to the effect of the words you use.

Chapter 8. *What is Really Important in Life?*—How much conscious thought have you given to what is really important in your life? People diagnosed with life-challenging diseases are forced to face this question—you can do it without such circumstances.

Chapter 9. *Distance Writing, Structured Writing, and Workbooks*—Writing in a structured way can be a powerful agent of change. (Pennebaker and L'Abate are major proponents.)

Chapter 10. *The Importance of Family and Adopted Family*—Life is with people, and contact with family, friends, adopted family, and acquaintances is explored here.

Chapter 11. *Touch and Touching: A Dilemma?*—Making physical contact with psychotherapy clients has been treated as a no-no, but it has its place and can be amazingly helpful.

Chapter 12. *Chuckling and Laughter and Having Fun*—This chapter is based in part on an essay I wrote for a chemistry journal a long time ago (Battino, 1973) on the importance of having fun in teaching. Fun also has a place in therapy, especially the idea of being able to chuckle at one's self and others.

Chapter 13. *Inclusivity: Either/Or vs. Both/And*—This is an oxymoronic approach developed by Bill O'Hanlon that scrambles a client's thinking in helpful ways.

Chapter 14. *Eye Movement Approaches*—Reading eye movements, as in the NLP eye accessing cues manner, can be quite helpful. Working with eye movements using EMDR or EMI can be effective with clients who have PTSD.

Chapter 15. *Cognitive Hypnotherapy and the Three Gifts*—Cognitive hypnotherapy was developed by Trevor Silvester and has much to offer. A few aspects of his work are illustrated here.

Chapter 16. *Transforming Negative Self-Talk*—This chapter summarizes some of the work in Steve Andreas's new book (Andreas, 2012) on transforming negative self-talk. Since we see many clients whose lives are limited by this kind of talk, Andreas's exercises and ideas can be quite useful.

Chapter 17. *On the Importance of Non-Importance—The "Nonesuch"*—What is really important in what clients tell you *and* what happens in a therapy session? Is therapy effective?

Chapter 18. *Behavior Modification*—In a way, you can consider all psychotherapy interventions to be behavior modification. Some of the classical methods will be reviewed here.

Chapter 19. *Gestalt Therapy*—Group work and linguistic patterns and interventions like the two-chair approach are discussed. (This is based on the pioneering work of Fritz Perls.)

Chapter 20. *Bioenergetic Analysis*—Alexander Lowen's ideas about body work and its connection to psychotherapy have things to teach us.

Chapter 21. *Neurolinguistic Programming (NLP)*—According to NLP, there are many ways of working with people primarily based on the clever use of language and how the mind works.

Chapter 22. *Encounter Groups and Group Therapy*—This is where it all started in the 60s and 70s. Group therapy is not used much anymore, yet it is one of the best ways to work with people individually and in a group/social setting.

Chapter 23. *First- and Second-Order Change and Reframing*—Reframing (content and context) is the preferred mode of bringing about *second-order change,* which is the most effective kind.

Chapter 24. *Ideomotor Signaling*—Working with questions using ideomotor signaling is a rapid way to get to the root(s) of concerns and resolve them.

Chapter 25. *Psychodrama*—Jakob and Zerka Moreno were the pioneers of psychodrama, which in a group setting can lead to rapid and profound changes in people.

Chapter 26. *Solution-Focused Brief Therapy*—Solution-focused therapy is a 180° paradigmatic shift from problem-oriented approaches.

Chapter 27. *Narrative Therapy*—Developed by Michael White and David Epston and involves personal narratives and the community.

Chapter 28. *Hypnosis*—There are many uses of hypnosis in psychotherapy. (Milton H. Erickson almost single-handedly brought hypnosis into repute and practice and developed endless uses of it in the twentieth century.)

Chapter 29. *Provocative Therapy*—An intriguing approach developed by Frank Farrelly which can be quite powerful when you are stuck in working with a client.

Part III is simply a concluding section with some final thoughts about what has preceded.

Chapter Two

Expectation:
The Essence of Brief Therapy

2.1 Introduction

My interest in the power of expectation in doing very brief therapy (or any length of therapy) began with a presentation by Steve de Shazer in which he talked about an experiment they had performed at the Brief Family Therapy Center of Milwaukee (BFTC). As I recall, their receptionist was instructed, upon reviewing the intake form for whoever dropped into their facility, to tell the clients one of two things. The first client was told, "For what you have written down here it typically takes five sessions for our therapists to help people." The next client was told, "For what you have written down here it typically takes about ten sessions for our staff to help people." This information was coded so that the therapist did not know who was told five sessions and who was told ten sessions. About a year later they examined the staff notes for the five- and ten-session clients. What they found was that the ten-session clients typically started doing significant work on their concerns in the eighth or ninth session. For the five-session clients, significant work started in the fourth session. This was a remarkable outcome. Being a "hard" scientist (physical chemistry) I immediately graphed these results and extrapolated down to zero sessions! That is not feasible, of course. So, why not tell all clients that you are a very brief therapist who rarely sees clients more than one or two times? You consider that each session is the last one, although your agreement with the client is that they can come back for as many sessions as they feel are being helpful. I have functioned in this mode ever since.

My clients know either from other people or directly from me that this is the way I work. Therefore, my expectation (and that of the client) is that change can come about very rapidly, and usually in one session. Since I work for myself and my office is in my home I am free to ignore the clock and the sessions are as long as needed. I do not accept insurance for a variety of reasons: (1) to avoid the paperwork; (2) to avoid the necessity of making a diagnosis and a treatment plan (do you need one for a single session?); and (3) to keep my fee lower than would be necessary to share some with the insurance people. It also turns out that in these circumstances I am exempt from the HIPPA requirements! My office is in my home, and since I see few clients (by choice) there is no need for parking or a receptionist, etc. The fee is low partly because that is what Erickson did, and partly because I have adequate pension plans. This is certainly a nice way to work.

2.2 Single-Session Therapy

Over the years the therapist's expectation of the number of needed sessions (dependent on the therapist's orientation and model) has declined from the years of weekly sessions that Freud's followers started out with to the insurance mandated number of sessions assigned to particular diagnoses. The latter seem to run between eight and twelve. Of course, if you are in private practice, there can be economic and marketing considerations. I do assume that we are all ethical professionals and that the aforementioned considerations are rarely abused.

The modern era of single-session therapy (SST) can be thought of as starting with *Single Session Therapy* by Moshe Talmon. At the time he was working at Kaiser Permanente in the Bay Area, where he had access to their extensive records. (It should be noted that Michael F. Hoyt and Robert Rosenbaum were Talmon's collaborators on that project.) There were three rather surprising things that Talmon found: (1) the most frequent (modal) length of therapy for every one of the therapists was one; (2) in a period of one year, thirty per cent of all patients chose to come for only one session; and (3) a follow-up study showed that there was essentially no correlation between what the client stated helped them and what the therapist thought was helpful in that single session. Also, there was no correlation involving the therapist's theoretical orientation. A relevant quote from Talmon's book (p. 11) is:

> In most of the SST cases where patients reported particu-
> larly successful outcomes, the therapist appeared to have
> conducted a rather simple, dull session. In fact, in many
> successful SSTs, it is the patient who appears to be in con-
> trol and sets the pace for change.

This quote contains much food for thought about how we con-
duct sessions!

Given the study by de Shazer and his colleagues and Talmon's
book (and his collaborators), why is it that therapists do not strive
for SST? In the de Shazer, et al. study, the expectation of the facility (and implied expectation of the therapists) was central to the
outcomes. In Talmon's study the controlling factor was that the client somehow found one session to be all that was needed. Talmon
almost wonderingly comments on this as follows (p. 65):

> Yet it is undeniable that a considerable number of patients
> are capable of recovering "against all odds" in ways that
> are very difficult to explain using plausible and logical
> thinking within traditional theories.

This quote speaks to the resilience and capacity of people to
change *on their own*. To this end we can cite a fascinating study by
Weiner-Davis, de Shazer and Gingerich (1987), in which they found
that when clients were asked about beneficial or useful changes
that had occurred between making their appointment and the appointment itself, most clients reported useful changes! From this
perhaps surprising result, the implication is that all therapists
should ask about changes occurring between the appointment and
its scheduling.

2.3 Expectation and the Placebo Effect

In my book on guided imagery (Battino, 2000) there is an entire
chapter on the placebo effect. When I started writing that book I
wondered if the usefulness of guided imagery was connected to the
placebo effect, and I had planned on writing a short section. Then
I dug into the literature and found many books and thousands
of articles. It was obvious to me that I had to devote more space
to this fascinating phenomenon. Is the thesis of this chapter—the

importance of expectation—also connected to the placebo effect? After all, it is the *expectation* of both the clinician and the client that this inert harmless substance or procedure will have beneficial effects physically and/or mentally. Indeed, one definition of the placebo effect is the nonspecific psychological or psychophysiological therapeutic effect produced by a placebo. Note that in the mental health field the emphasis is on the psychological effect.

A. K. Shapiro and his wife E. Shapiro (both physicians) did the earliest thorough study of the placebo effect. In their book (Shapiro and Shapiro, 1997) they made this remarkable statement (p. 2): **"...until recently the history of medical treatment was essentially the history of the placebo effect."** I have bold-faced this statement to indicate how important it is. They were basically stating that until the 1950s, with the advent of double-blind studies for medications and treatments, there was little or no scientific evidence that what doctors had been doing for millennia worked. Of course, people knew from ancient times that opium (in many forms) alleviated pain, but there were no controlled studies on purity and dosage. Folk medicine via drugs and ceremonies were effective more by belief than by controlled studies. People just *expected* that what they took or did, or what the native healer or shaman did, would work.

The ancient idea that illness (physical or mental) is caused by the possession of evil spirits continues to this day. Psychoanalysis was based on removing or understanding hidden causes and purgatives, emetics, enemas, bleeding, expectorants, and sudorifics (sweat-inducing) were the treatments of choice. Trephining (drilling a hole in the skull) to let out evil spirits has a modern equivalent (though much better controlled now) in convulsive shock therapy. Again, if you believed the possession model, then it was frequently the case that these treatments worked.

If expectation is effectively synonymous with the placebo effect, the practitioner's dilemma is how to use expectation and placebos ethically. If I say to a prospective client, "I rarely see clients more than one or two times," is that statement sufficiently waffled that there are no guarantees, but that this is the norm in my practice? Can the medical doctor say, "This treatment has worked well with most of my clients even though it is still under study"? In the early part of the twentieth century, and before that, pharmaceutical houses carried placebos in their catalogues. These placebos came in many sizes, shapes, and colors. Considering an aspirin as a standard size pill, modern studies have shown that if the placebo is significantly smaller *or* larger than an aspirin that the placebo effect is greater. (Placebo injections are more potent than pills!)

Incidentally, some refer to the idea of expectation in therapy as "priming" or "seeding" or "lining up the ducks."

2.4 Nocebo, Nosocomial, and Iatrogenic Effects

In writing about the placebo effect we would be remiss to not mention the opposite—*the nocebo effect.* This occurs when the treatment or message is harmful to the person. There have been, of course, medical treatments that have been harmful. The old favorite treatment of bleeding, for example, just weakened the person who lost blood. At one time a radical mastectomy was the treatment of choice for a woman who had breast cancer. This is not currently the preferred surgical intervention for most women with breast cancer.

The most common nocebo is a "hex" or "witch" or negative message given to children by significant people in their lives as they are growing up: "You will never succeed." "What an ugly duckling." "You are just bad." "Why don't you ever get anything right?" The intent is mostly non-malignant, but definitely ill-informed. Remember, the meaning of any message is not your intent, but how it is received. Words are *not* harmless. (I have written a book about healing language (Battino, 2011).) These negative messages are remembered and incorporated into the way we think and feel about ourselves. They can have profound effects on our lives for a very long time.

Reversing or eliminating a nocebo message can take considerable skill on the part of a therapist. One way is to add perspective by realizing that you are quite a different person now, one who has survived to this time, and one who has many more resources than that child had way back then. Another way is via forgiving the people who gave the message when as an older person you realize how fallible and human parents (and others) can be. When you forgive this frees you up—the forgiveness is primarily for you. There are cultures like the Australian Aborigines where "pointing the bone" can cause a person to die. Is this any different than a statement like, "All of the men in our family have died of heart attacks by the time they were sixty"? Careful...

A *nosocomial* illness is one caused by stays in hospitals or other health facilities. One can consider this to be of epidemic proportions when studies have shown that dying from these illnesses or mistakes is the second or third highest cause of death in the United States. This is of the order of 100,000 people per year! There are surgical and medication mistakes, but a common cause of death, illness, and readmission to hospitals (Medicare no longer pays for the latter) is hospital-acquired infections. These infections tend to be more virulent than those acquired outside hospitals since they tend to be more resistant to treatment. Five years ago when I was checking the hospitals in my area for their infection rates they were in the range of ten to thirteen per cent. This is a national tragedy for it has been well-known for a number of years that proper antisepsis and sanitation in hospitals can reduce this rate to one per cent or less. There are many examples of hospitals that have done this, the best example being the Planetree hospitals. It is now possible to go on the Internet and check out the infection rate of a hospital.

The term *iatrogenic* simply means "doctor-caused." Operating on the wrong limb or organ has become less frequent; however, there are still mistakes by health professionals with regard to surgery and medications. The practice of computerizing data for patients is minimizing this problem, but still the conventional advice is to stay in a hospital or medical facility for as short a time as possible. Long-term stays, like at nursing homes and rehabilitation facilities, need to be approached with caution, and their infection rates should be checked. There will always be mistakes. As Forrest Gump aptly stated (in a cleaned-up form), "Fecal matter happens." Be cautious. In fairness I should point out that these are not malevolent actions by health care professionals since I believe they are really caring and well-trained and aware and have our best interests in mind.

2.5 Expecting the Unexpected

How many of us are open to change? My friend Carl Hammer-schlag, M.D., is a superb motivational speaker. One of his themes is that the only people who do not change are dead. If you are alive, you are changing all of the time. There are cells in your body that are replaced within minutes, and even your bones are regenerated every few years. Each breath, each heartbeat is part of this endless recycling and regeneration. There is that old observation that you cannot step into the same river twice. Yes, we do have habits and rituals, but do you actually brush your teeth the same way each day? Ask almost any wife and she will tell you that her husband resists change (my wife tells me this). And yet even I adapt and change, even though many of those small changes can be unnerving and disorienting. I heard Bernie Siegel opine at a lecture, "What would a visitor from Mars notice about what we do and how we do it?" Oh, to see ourselves as others see us!

If we expect and anticipate the unexpected, how different would our lives be? Would our lives be more interesting, productive, exciting, dangerous? Or would we find ways to settle once again into the humdrum of routines? We do have choices even within the physical, economic, social, and historical constraints that are both real and imaginary. Dare, experiment, explore…who knows what could happen?

With regard to expectation, the bottom line is that whatever you do as a therapist is more effective if you congruently believe in its ability to help your clients.

Chapter Three

The Power of Pauses in Hypnosis and Psychotherapy

3.1 Pause Power

I was on a topical panel at the December 2011 Erickson Congress in Phoenix, and the topic was hypnotic language. One of the ideas I presented was that novice hypnotists talk too much. This is particularly the case when they are conducting a hypnosis session. There is almost the conviction that when a client is in trance they are not allowed to talk! Is it okay to ask a client who is in trance a question? Would this break the trance? How can you tell if they are responding differently than in their waking state? Does it matter if they do respond differently? The safest thing to do must be to talk all of the time and not ask questions.'

I told the audience that for a while at these conferences I was in the habit of timing how long and how frequently well-known professionals paused when doing demonstrations with volunteers. When studying movies of Milton Erickson and listening to tapes of him I had noticed that he did not talk all of the time, and that he not only asked questions of clients in trance, but also held conversations with them. Consider that a pause of ten seconds in a conversation seems like a long time. A pause of one minute feels like it is lasting forever. Pauses are important in that they give the client time to process and ten react to the suggestions.

People come to see us because they are stuck. They feel that they cannot change, and that whatever they have tried (on their own or with other therapists) has not worked. Our job then is to change "I can't" to "I won't" and what they consider to be involuntary behavior to voluntary behavior. They are stuck essentially because some stimulus or factor in their environment invariably results in the *same* interpretation or the *same* response. This means that this single invariable response needs to be replaced by several realistic interpretations and/or behaviors. That is, to replace "stuck" with *choice*. Viktor Frankl (1984) taught us that we may have no control over what life deals out to us (in his case being in a concentration camp), but we always have the choice of how we respond. Realistically, what we can do in a given situation may be limited by circumstances. Our response then has to be in how we react and feel and think about the constraints that life and happenstance have placed upon us. In this regard we all have the capacity to choose.

If you are talking all of the time and throwing out possibilities of other responses (preferably metaphorically), then the client needs time to process and think about these new ideas. They will do this typically by not hearing what you are saying as they follow up on a suggestion. That is, they go on their merry way working out how they can realistically make that particular choice. After a while they hear you again. If you are very observant, you can pick up clues in their body language that they are off into their own world. Would it not be better to put many pauses in what you are saying so that they can have the time to pursue these ideas? Pause and observe. Ask if they would like some time to pursue an idea.

A digression—how much do we really know about the client in our office? We can take some notes about what troubles or concerns them. We can take notes about their personal history. We can observe and listen. They share this information with us for the few minutes they are in our office, an artificial atmosphere and place which is basically unrelated to their life. At most we can get a few ideas about them and their lives and what is possible and what is not. They tell us this in words which we translate via our own life experiences. However, only they really know the history and feelings associated with their lives. We can make educated guesses about various choices and possibilities for change. It is my hope that when I tell stories incorporating many possibilities my client will latch onto one or more of them that fits their unique life and circumstances. They then need time to elaborate on these possibilities in ways that are realistic to them. The more specific the possibilities I mention, the less chance that they will find something useful. The more vague and poetic I am in what I say, the greater the likelihood that they will find something they can build on in their own unique way. This means that we are fumbling in the dark and hoping they will make sense out of these stories. It is my expectation that my clients will discover useful choices. *They need the time to do so.*

At the topical panel I mentioned timing Ernest L. Rossi in a number of his demonstrations. I was astounded to find that Rossi used so many pauses, and that some of the pauses lasted minutes. How many of us have that kind of patience? Rossi is also a master of reading body language, and he could gauge when to interject with a comment or new ideas.

Pauses can make for effective therapy and communication. So, I will pause here before writing the next chapter!

Chapter Four

Poetry in Hypnosis and Psychotherapy

4.1 Introduction

At the topical panel I mentioned above, Steven Gilligan and I both talked about the uses of poetry in hypnosis. In my book on metaphors there is a section on poetry (Battino, 2002, pp. 44–50). About eighty years ago, Snyder wrote a book on hypnotic poetry primarily from the viewpoint of a poet. Mostly he was writing about the characteristics that make recited poetry hypnotic in nature in terms of "mesmerizing" an audience. There are six characteristics that such poems have in common, and they are listed below with page references to Snyder's book:

1. An unusually perfect pattern of sound, which tends to be soothing. "Hypnotic poems in general give us heavy stresses falling regularly at half-second intervals, and so ornamented that the rhythmically inclined listener has his attention drawn to the sound rather than the sense." (p. 42)
2. In these poems there is a freedom from abrupt changes which can break the spell, and this especially means freedom from ideas that might compel mental alertness.
3. There is a certain vagueness of imagery in these poems. "The pictures presented in these hypnotic poems have such soft, shadowy outlines that one may fill in the details to suit one's fancy or let the picture remain hazy. They foster an idle, dreamy state of consciousness like the preliminary stage of hypnosis." (p. 42)

4. There are fatigue-producing elements. "Paradoxical though it sounds, we may yet have to accept the view that in the early stages of a hypnotic poem, a foreign word, an obscure phrase, or any slight difficulty that causes fatigue from strain on the part of the listener may actually promote the ultimate aesthetic effect at which the artist aims." (p. 45)

5. Another characteristic is the use of a refrain or a frequent repetition (like "nevermore" in Edgar Allen Poe's "The Raven").

6. Importantly, these hypnotic poems tend to use *suggestion* on the entranced listener, and the suggestions may have a post-hypnotic effect. The suggestion usually comes near the end of the poem after "there has been a long preliminary soothing of the listener's senses by monotonous rhythmic 'passes'." (p. 48)

Wow. These characteristics will hopefully influence you into incorporating poetry into your hypnotic work, especially items 3 and 6. English is a wonderful language since there are so many meaningful and useful words that have multiple meanings and are also ambiguous, such as love, hand, change, store, turn, talk, feel, ship, sense, sit, move, pen, hope, really, and belief. There are also many words in English that exhibit phonological ambiguity in that they are pronounced the same, but are different words. Here are some examples: know/no, rite/write/right, wait/weight, wade/weighed, way/weigh, knew/new, knot/not, and to/too/two. These puzzling words can be slipped into an induction or into the body of a metaphor to add confusion and choice.

4.2 Some Examples of Poetry Usage

At the aforementioned panel discussion, I took a point of privilege and quoted Robert Frost's "Fire and Ice."

> Some say the world will end in fire.
> Some say in ice.
> From what I've tasted of desire
> I hold with those who favor fire.
> But if it had to perish twice
> I think that ice is also great
> and would suffice.

There is enough ambiguity in this poem to almost force the listener to join the debate about fire and desire and ice and sufficiency.

Here let me cite with commentary some of my favorite Robert Frost poems, and I hope you have a collection of favorite poems and parts of poems.

"The Road Not Taken" is about someone who has a choice in going down one path or another. The poet ends up taking the path he perceived was less traveled on, and finds that doing so has made all the difference in his life. Yet, earlier in the poem Frost notes that he cannot really see any differences in the two paths. It is fascinating to note that when you are faced with choices in your life and you make a particular decision, you almost always find good reasons for that decision being the best choice.

"Mending Wall" begins by stating that there is something not lovable in a wall, and that this "something" wants the wall to fall down and disappear. The poem continues with thoughts about walls—one of them being that this particular wall between two farms actually serves no purpose! You may then wish to ask yourself about the walls and boundaries in your life that may have served a purpose at one time, but no longer do. How have you boxed and walled yourself in? Are those walls removable, and how can you move outside of that box?

Frost had a superb eye for Nature, and in "Birches" noted that they can easily sway in the wind. In his imagination he sees a boy swinging on one, and then wonders what being a "swinger of birches" would be like. The imagery in a poem like this can regress us back to childhood and teen states where we can relive or imagine now that freedom to swing.

The poem "Precaution" is a reflection on how when he was young that Frost never dared to be radical. And, this was because he feared it would make him conservative when he was old.

What an interesting way he and we (in our own ways) may have restricted ourselves! This poem reminded me of a lecture on the life of the German poet Goethe I heard when I was a college student, and which I have never forgotten. We were told that when Goethe was young he decided to make his own life his life's work, and that he got progressively more radical as he aged. How many of us are now more daring or "radical" than when we were young?

I generally use poetic language and imagery towards the end of a hypnosis session. This has usually been preceded by a story or a variety of suggestions couched within personal experiences or within "I had a client who..." or "Someone once said..."

These little images are stream of consciousness with many pauses. There is no introduction to these images and I just slide into saying them. Here is an example:

> ...a lazy floating cloud...a baby's smile...that blade of grass...a raindrop...an insect buzzing...the wind in the trees...a glass of cold water on a hot day...that smile...a touch...the sound of water in a stream...holding a hand...being   lazy...thunder...laughing...joy...the moon in the morning...a leaf fluttering down in the fall...buds in the spring...reading to a child...that flower...the odor of fresh baked bread...a secret smile...

Just let your mind wander, return to something from the beginning of the hypnosis session, and perhaps wind up with, "And now, taking a deep breath or two, blinking your eyes, and perhaps stretching, return to this room here and now. Thank you."

Poetry can enhance what you do and fill your heart and that of your clients.

Chapter Five

Dreams, Hopes, and Unfulfilled Desires

5.1 In General

My volunteer work for over one score of years has been with people who have life-challenging diseases. I make distinctions between disease and illness, curing and healing. A *disease* is the physical manifestation of something that is wrong with the body. Diseases are infections, broken bones, cancer, diabetes, etc. Medical doctors are quite skilled at curing diseases. That is, *curing* restores the body to health. Broken bones are fixed, infections disappear, and cancers go into remission. An *illness*, on the other hand, is how we *feel* and *think* about the disease. Thoughts and feelings about a disease are things we learn from our families and cultures. In some traditions the patient is expected to always be stoic, while in others the patient is expected to be openly emotional. Since an illness involves emotions and attitudes an illness can be *healed* by changing the way we feel and think. Do you perceive a partially filled glass of water as half full or half empty? Do you have hope or are you pessimistic? It is interesting to note that the literature on psycho-neuroimmunology and mind/body interactions points to the observation that healing can sometimes result in curing. The work of the psychologist Lawrence LeShan speaks to this.

In his books (LeShan, 1974, 1977, 1982, 1989), LeShan shares three reasons that a person typically gives for wanting not to die:

1. They fear the circumstances of death or dying, i.e. pain, the unknown, helplessness.

2. They want to live for others, helping the others attain their goals.
3. They want to live their own life, to be able to sing their own unique song.

With respect to these reasons, LeShan states (1982, p. 139):

> For reasons I do not fully understand, the body will not mobilize its resources for either or both of the first two reasons. Only for the third will the self-healing and self-recuperative abilities of the individual come strongly into play. When individuals with cancer understand this and begin to search for and fight for their own special music in ways of being, relating, working, creating, they tend to begin to respond more positively…

This conclusion by LeShan, which is based on his personal experience with many terminal cancer patients, points to the importance of hopes and dreams and dealing with unfinished business in healing. Singing your own unique song reverberates with Joseph Campbell's recommendation of "finding your bliss" and Viktor Frankl's "finding meaning in your life." (You may also be interested in a recent book by LeShan (2012) where his attempt to define "consciousness" is both fascinating and challenging.)

So, when I work with people who have life-challenging diseases (please note that I do not use the phrase "life-threatening disease" since this has negative connotations), I always ask about their hopes and dreams, particularly those from their childhood and youth. In LeShan's book *Cancer as a Turning Point* (LeShan, 1989, pp. 48–54) he tells the story of Minnie, an older woman who is dying of cancer. She eventually tells him of a childhood passion for the ballet. LeShan arranges for her to get books and magazines and articles about the ballet. From being a "model patient" (docile) she now is devouring everything she can read about ballet. He even arranges for a prima ballerina to visit with her. Minnie surges back to life to the surprise of the staff and her family. Sadly, a heat wave hits New York City in the era before air conditioning and she dies. I read Minnie's story when I do presentations about guided imagery and healing and the power of providing access to a person's hopes and dreams in some way. These are the fantasies and daydreams we have while we are growing up, and they never leave us.

When I was growing up I loved opera and dreamed about being an opera singer. I have a big untrained voice, and did not start into music until I was 45 years old. There was a period of three years when I took voice lessons and could sing operatic arias. Unfortunately, I did not develop an ear for music and was never sure I was singing the right notes! This was frustrating, to say the least. I gave up the voice lessons, but I had attained my dream of singing opera, no matter for how short a time and no matter in what limited ways. (Another dream was to be a writer and I have published a great deal, including poetry and plays and many scientific papers.) Do I have more dreams? Yes.

The point I am making is that it is important as a therapist, a counselor, or a friend to elicit these hopes and dreams. If at all possible, help to facilitate them in whatever way is realistically appropriate in the present. My mother-in-law, Ellie Ridinger, lived to almost 94. As a girl she wanted to engage in sports. After retiring she got into swimming and Senior Olympics on the local and national scene. When she was 91 she won one gold medal and two silver medals at the Louisville National Senior Olympics. At her memorial service we had a display of her medals and the T-shirts she owned from all of her past competitions. It is never too late.

5.2 Unfinished Business and End of Life Considerations

At the time of writing I am 82 years old and my wife of 53 years is 77. We are blessed with good health, vigor, and mental capacity. We are also concerned about the fact that as people age they slow down and frequently end up with physical and mental disabilities. So, we are planning ahead on how we will cope with probable debility as we age. Our house is one story and that is good. It is not within walking distance of the center of town with its stores and the library and the movie house, and that is not good. There is a good independent living facility where we live, but it is too far from the center of town for easy access. Since we do not want to leave here for another location, we are working on ways of perhaps buying a smaller house closer to the center of town. We have living wills, durable powers of attorney for health, powers of attorney, wills, long-term care insurance, and pre-paid funeral arrangements if we die locally or at some distance. We have written about the disposition of our ashes and the design of a memorial service. And, quite importantly, we have talked with our sons and their wives about our wishes. We do not plan on dying any time soon and we both have long-lived relatives. Still, one needs to think about these things in advance and to plan for them. An alternative which many take is not to be bothered with all of this and to just let the kids take care of things. That alternative is hostile and uncaring. We are fortunate that at the present palliative care and hospice programs are almost universal. We also have caring and compassionate medical doctors.

Unfinished business primarily has to do with relationships and not with practical matters like finances. It is amazing how many people we interact with and know of who hold grudges and are angry with relatives and friends for years and generations. Many people do not know how to forgive and forget and move on. Forgiving someone is mostly clearing out debris and garbage for the person doing the forgiving and not for the person forgiven. Let go of all that accumulated junk. Because I did or said something recently or decades ago, it need not make life unbearable now and continue to hurt. I believe that many people blame their parents or teachers or significant others in their lives for "causing" or "making" them into who they are now. I had such feelings about my parents. It was not until my late thirties that I had a freeing revelation. This was the recognition that my parents, as all of us, were fallible human beings. I am an optimist and believe that most people are good at heart and do not consciously do malicious things. Parents make mistakes like we all do. Not even saints are perfect. So, find ways of reconnecting with those who we feel have harmed us, find ways of giving up the grudges, and find ways to love and be loved. Life is with people—we cannot do without each other. If your efforts to forgive, forget, and reconnect fail, then you can be sad about that and just continue your own life.

Ira Byock has written a loving book entitled *The Four Things That Matter Most: A Book About Living* (Byock, 2004). (Also see Byock, 1997.) He recommends that towards the end of your life you communicate five things to the significant people in your life. They are:

> Please forgive me.
> I forgive you.
> I love you.
> Thank you.
> Goodbye.

I would add a sixth statement, which is, "I forgive myself." Please be aware that you do not have to wait until death is close or imminent to say these things!

LIFE IS WITH PEOPLE

Chapter Six

Chatting as Therapy

6.1 Introduction

I have been more or less conventionally trained in a variety of approaches. One of them, Bioenergetic Analysis, required physically manipulating clients and I did not get into that. However, the training sessions in bioenergetics were beneficial to me and the other trainees (as is often the case). In Part II of this book I will be writing about some of the approaches I was trained in that seem to have gone by the board over the years, but which I feel continue to have much to offer. Conventional training provides us with many interventions, that is, things to do in a session. The NLP people have been the most prolific in designing useful and clever interventions. It really is useful to know many different ways of working with clients. There is a principle in cybernetics that states, "In any complex interaction, the component with the most variability controls." A session with a client certainly qualifies as a complex interaction, so it behooves you to have more variability than your client. (The so-called "therapist killers" who are more experienced as clients than many of us are as therapists frequently control sessions!)

The common descriptive of "intervention" implies control and manipulation on the part of the therapist. Clients come to us because they are stuck and expect us to intervene and manipulate. Otherwise, how can change occur? In observing someone like Ernest L. Rossi do demonstrations with volunteers at conferences I have been impressed by his minimalist manner. He appears to work as a gentle, observant, and totally with-the-client guide. He does operate out of a theoretical base, yet the session appears to be a seamless interaction between two people where one of them throws out occasional comments and suggestions. There is a lot of listening and pausing. A cognitive behavioral therapist (using CBT) also operates out of a theoretical base, but the approach seems to me to be much more directive and obtrusive and "I know what is good for you" than what Rossi does. I mention all of this here in the introduction to this chapter so you know where I am coming from as I describe in the next section what I do as "chatting."

6.2 Chatting

Over the years (I got my MS degree in counseling in 1978) I have evolved into a way of working with clients that I describe as "chatting." I deliberately use the word "evolved" since this was a slow transformation. A few days ago I met with a client who was referred to me as someone who had many concerns and who had been to see many different therapists over the years. She wanted to see someone different. So, we chatted for over ninety minutes. She told me about many of the things that had been troubling her. I listened attentively, giving her indications that I was actually hearing what she was saying (rather than thinking about what I was going to say or do next!). I was sure she felt heard and valued. So, we chatted about this and that. We had some common interests and experiences and connected via them. With respect to one of her concerns I gave a mini history of how therapy has changed over the years from working for a long time with a client individually and whose concern may have been marital or familial, to couples therapy and family therapy and extended family therapy, and back to working singly by "inserting" or "injecting" the client back into their life system as a *change agent*. I could have just gone directly to discussing *change agent* possibilities. Instead, she now knew something about how what I was going to suggest worked. I was still the "expert." The difference in this way of interacting is that we were now working *collaboratively*. We were also having fun thinking about various possibilities. And, she would be able to choose something that was appropriate to her situation. After all, she knew the people involved and I only knew them via hearsay. This congenial way of being together ranged over a number of other possible things she could do and feel and think about from a different perspective. We were in this together. Since I love the Miracle Question (see page 153 (26.2)),

I slipped that in at an appropriate time. She played with that a bit and then we moved on. I could have forced the issue and continued with the Miracle Question approach—you need to follow the client's lead—this comes out of really being *with* them.

What is this "chatting" stuff all about? I am not much into theory guiding what I do. After all, the literature is full of endless theories about how and why people do what they do. When what you do is theory-driven your range of options becomes limited by the theory! If eye movements are the entry to the soul and the psyche and internal operations, then it is effectively incumbent upon you to use interventions involving eye movement. If I have singled this out here, it is not because I do not know that eye movement has been used successfully by therapists with many clients. Eye movement is but one example. In the context of theory-driven approaches, I am reminded of a statement that Bill O'Hanlon likes to quote, namely, "Whenever I feel a hypothesis coming on, I lie down until it goes away." This is *your* educated guess. So, I am atheoretical.

But I must have a theory! I am sure there are those who say that having no theory is having a theory which is that no theory is needed! So be it. I do have expectations. One of them is that I will be able to help whoever comes to see me, and that I will be able to do so within a relatively small number of sessions. Another is that we will be able to make human contact and that the chat will naturally ensue. Much has been written about the "therapeutic alliance" and chatting could be described by that phrase. I like to think of chatting as two individual and unique human beings spending some time together listening to each other and talking about their lives. Life can involve periods of intense loneliness, isolation, hopelessness, and helplessness. Making contact with another person and sharing these feelings of frustration can be freeing. Here is someone who, at least for this meeting, is really with me. There are no distractions. We talk, we share, we explore possibilities. I am not "doing" stuff with you or to you. Perhaps I take on the role of a trusted friend, uncle, grandparent, parent. (Being almost invariably older and grayer than my clients helps.) The client can think of me in whatever way he wishes. We chat in this isolated artificial environment of my TV room (my "consulting" room and office for sessions) which is separate from their everyday lives. In these chats I do more self-disclosure than many would feel to be proper and/or comfortable doing. If my client is sharing information about her life, it would be strange in this kind of intimate setting for me to be analytically aloof. Then I would be a technician and not a person.

Since my clients know that I use hypnosis (if it makes sense to do so), most of my sessions end with hypnosis. I weave into my hypnotic language themes and ideas that have arisen earlier in the session. Stories are sometimes told, since everyone likes stories, and within the metaphors may be possible thoughts and actions and possibilities that the client will latch onto. Almost every one of these hypnotic interludes ends with poetic images as a kind of coda to connect the client with Nature and warm fuzzy memories and feelings. In a way, this can be considered to be a comforting confusion time.

I recently read a book by Hillary and Bradford Keeney (Keeney and Keeney, 2012) that struck me as illustrating their way of chatting with clients. From a complex book with many case studies, examples and historical analyses I am just going to cite two quotes:

> Rest assured that therapy is a form of improvisational theater and belongs in the house of the performing arts. (p. 9)
> The embodied circular loop of improvisation is the most respectful relationship possible with a client for it utilizes whatever the client and therapist bring and then utilizes what happens next in the interaction. We call this "circular therapeutics" and regard it as the key to bringing a healing heart to therapy. (p. 41)

Circular therapeutics is based on the work of Gregory Bateson, and the authors cite his work and his thinking throughout. In the case studies I was struck by the seeming similarity of their approach to what I have described above as "chatting." Given their background and experience in many healing environments and cultures, it appeared to me that what could be described as intuition was really an extraordinary awareness of the other person as a unique human being in an exceptional one-on-one interaction. The resulting conversation or chat between these two people was manifested in what the Keeneys call the "healing heart." So, there are many ways to "chat."

Chatting is my style, I am comfortable with it, and it seems to work with the people who come to visit with me. Will it work for you? Evolution contains surprises and I do not know where this process will end for me. Let's have a chat some time…

Chapter Seven

On the Importance of
Healing Language

7.1 Introduction

I've written a whole book about this (Battino, 2011) and this chapter will summarize what I believe is important to know about healing language. The bottom line is that not only do words matter, how you say them also matters. There is a story about Milton Erickson who was fascinated in his youth by hearing a performer at a county fair say the word "no" in more than thirty different ways. How many ways can you think of? What are the impacts of each of those ways? No can be said from the extremes of anger and delight. I used to say, "I never give up hope." I now say, "I always have hope." The motto of the cancer support group I facilitate is, "You may have to believe the diagnosis. You do not have to believe the prognosis." This motto is one example of healing language. Another is the switch in talking about the group as being one for people who have life-*challenging* diseases (rather than life-threatening). The word "challenge" opens doors while the word "threatening" closes doors. Similarly, I never make psychological diagnoses since for most people a diagnosis locks a person into a rigid place and closes off opportunities for change. (If I had to make a diagnosis it would be that the person is *temporarily troubled* where "temporary" means the "trouble" is time-limited.) Problems are more difficult to resolve.

We do not generally consider listening to be language. Yet the most healing thing you can generally do is to *really* listen to someone. That is, listening appears to be the *passive* part of a conversation even though it involves active participation for both people.

Knowing that what you are saying is being heard is healing. Compliance with a doctor's (or other health professional's) directions is a major concern. For example, the prescribed regimen for adult onset diabetes is well-established and has a proven outcome record. Yet the literature indicates that perhaps only 50% of those with this disease follow the regimen and know precisely what to do. On occasion, we have taken voice recorders to sessions with doctors. In addition, my wife or I take notes. Written handouts are frequently not available or incomplete or difficult to interpret. (For me a wonderful recent exception was the packet of handouts given to me by my endodontist before he did some needed oral surgery.) This, of course, should be routine, and health professionals need to check that clients have heard what they have been told and have made notes about what to do. Let me expand on this with respect to diagnoses of serious and life-challenging diseases.

When I have been given a diagnosis about something that is going to involve an invasive procedure I tend to not hear most of what is said, and I go into a kind of stasis or zombie state. Some examples of that are needing a TURP (transurethral resection of the prostate), a total knee replacement, oral surgery, and a "routine" colonoscopy. For various lengths of time before each of these procedures (which all came out well) I was just "not there," and in a state where I felt like I was holding my breath all of the time. None of these procedures were life-threatening ones (although they were challenging). Yet, even with my experience and everything that I read and my ability to use self-hypnosis the dissociation was there. When the diagnosis is something like cancer the dissociation and distancing and withdrawal and reactions are much stronger. Patients and health professionals need to be acutely aware of the effect of a diagnosis and how to use healing language in such circumstances. When they are overly optimistic and hopeful, i.e. saying "positive" things, this can sometimes be counterproductive. That is, in those circumstances cheering up can sound false and be disturbing. Healing language starts with empathy and caring that shows that the physician understands and has some sense of what is going on in the patient's mind, some sensitivity to their emotions. This can be followed by supportive statements about how the physician will be available to the patient and stick with them.

In the next section I will discuss healing language for surgery, and in the following section give a few scenarios from my book on healing language.

7.2 Healing Language for Surgery[1]

There are two things that I do to prepare people for surgery. The first is to have one or more individual sessions with the person to find out how they think/feel about surgery, what their past experiences may have been, and to gather enough information to make a helping/healing CD for them. The second is to prepare a set of comments they can give to their surgeon to make during the surgery itself. They will be discussed separately.

After obtaining information with respect to past surgeries and their experience with them, it is time to explore how they feel about the upcoming surgery. Are they fearful, and of what? This discussion may include the two common kinds of anesthesia: general and spinal (or local, if appropriate). There is evidence that general anesthesia and the drugs given along with it can have long-lasting effects of up to several months. For elderly patients this can frequently lead to dementia and confusion and dissociation, some of which can be long-lasting. This is serious and has to be anticipated for older patients. Depending on the surgery there are pros and cons for the different anesthetics and these need to be explored with the anesthesiologist well in advance of the surgery.

We explore whether they have had experience with relaxation or meditation or hypnosis, and this is discussed. There is a practice hypnosis session (people know I use hypnosis for surgery preparation). I ask about a "safe haven" or a place which is real or imaginary where they can go to in their mind before, during, and after the procedure. This practice "calibrating" hypnosis session lasts 25–30 minutes (as will the CD) and contains the following elements:

- Induction and relaxation (usually via counting breaths)
- Drifting off within their mind to the safe haven (which is described in some detail using *their* words)
- Pre-surgery relaxation comments
- Healing and relaxation comments for during surgery
- Healing and relaxation comments for post surgery recovery

---

1. Chapter 10 in my book on guided imagery (Battino, 2000, pp. 149–162) will be used as the resource for this section. (Due to an oversight when writing the book on healing language no mention was made of healing language for surgery.)

- Healing and relaxation comments for returning to a regular hospital room
- Healing and relaxation comments for after returning home

The basic approach is to establish *post-hypnotic* suggestions along the lines listed above. They can begin at whatever time they feel is most appropriate, i.e. on the way to the hospital, during the pre-op preparation, or on the way to the OR. The comments generally involve a *dissociation* to the safe haven, a place where they can stay and from which they can occasionally view what is going on with them "over there." They are told that their surgical team is experienced and expert and that they are safe in their hands. After the practice session they are asked if anything needs to be modified before the CD is made. It is recommended that they start listening to the CD one to two weeks before the surgery and as frequently as they feel it is helpful. Once they have the CD and have listened to it they can tell me if it meets their needs or should be modified in some way. If it's the latter, then a new CD is prepared. Some people make arrangements to listen to the CD or their own special music during the surgery.

There is significant evidence[2] that patients can hear what is said in the OR even when they are in the surgical plane of anesthesia. Since this is the case, I prepare a letter to their surgeon explaining this and the fact that their patient has been consulting with me to prepare for the surgery. This letter recommends that the surgeon or someone in the OR makes the following statements to the patient during the surgery (these should be tailored to the particular surgery and client). So that the patient knows the statement is directed to them, each statement is prefaced by their name and ends with "thank you." These statements are printed in bold-face and are pasted to a 5x8" index card which is then laminated or sealed in plastic.

- Mary—please slow down (or stop) the bleeding where I am working. Thank you.
- Mary—please relax your muscles in this area. Thank you.

---

2. See Pearson, 1961; Cheek, 1959, 1960a, 1960b, 1961, 1964, 1965, 1966, 1981; Rossi and Cheek, 1998, pp. 113–130; Dubin and Shapiro, 1974; Liu, Standen and Aitkenhead, 1992; Clawson and Swade, 1975; and Bank, 1985.

- Mary—this is going very well. Thank you.
- Mary—you will heal surprisingly quickly. Thank you.
- Mary—you will be surprisingly comfortable and at ease after this. Thank you.
- Mary—your recovery will be very rapid. Thank you.

My doctors have cooperated with me concerning these statements. (With local or spinal anesthetics I also give these messages to myself.) The people I have prepared in this way have all found this to be helpful.

7.3 Some Healing Scenarios

There are some sixty-eight scenarios in my healing language book (Battino, 2011). Appendix B (pp. 207–209) contains a smaller selection of key scenarios. Here are six of them:

Scenario 1: Lung Cancer—A 40-year-old man who is a fitness fanatic, except for his smoking, develops lung cancer.
RESPONSE: It must be very hard to accept a serious illness when you feel so fit.

Scenario 2: Cancer in Remission—There is a significant chance it will recur in the next few years.
RESPONSE: It must be awful for you to be continuously worrying about a recurrence.

Scenario 4: Palliative Care—Patient is told there is nothing more that can be done for them medically.
RESPONSE: You must be very worried about your future since I just told you that at the present time there is nothing more we can do besides keep you comfortable.

Scenario 10: Inoperable Tumor—Test results show that the patient has an inoperable tumor.
RESPONSE: You know, I always have hope. There are some other treatments that have been helpful. We have some time to explore these options. There's a great deal we can do to help you through this and to keep you comfortable.

Scenario 14: Patient Died in the OR—Surgeon talks to the family in the waiting room.

RESPONSE: I don't know how to tell you this, but _____ has just died. There was an unexpected complication. We did everything we could. He/she died suddenly and peacefully. He/she talked about you all of the time. I am going to miss him/her, too.

Scenario 24: Pancreatic Cancer and End of Life—A 72-year-old patient is told that he has pancreatic cancer which has metastasized.

RESPONSE: This is serious since the cancer has metastasized and there are no treatments. You may wish to take advantage of the local hospice program—they are very good at keeping you comfortable and helping with family. You can call on me at any time and I will be available.

Language can heal. We have all had experiences when we have been hurt by malicious or unthinking words. And we have also all experienced the joy and relief that loving and healing words can have on us. There is always choice in how and what we say.

Chapter Eight

What is Really Important in Life?

8.1 Introduction

I heard Jean Houston once talking about a presentation she does on what is really important in life. After an introduction to the topic she asks audience members to write down what is **really** important in their life. Then she asks them to write down what is **really really** important in their life. Finally, she asks them to write down what is **really really really** important in their life. She has found that there are unplumbed depths to this question and that it needs to be repeated three times for people to get down to the most significant things in their lives, the things that are most meaningful.

Viktor Frankl (1984) has written and spoken passionately about man's search for meaning and his own search for meaning that was forced upon him when he was incarcerated in various concentration camps by the Nazis. I have been privileged to meet Frankl a number of times, and have read most of his books, listened to many recordings, and viewed many videos. When I wrote my biography of him in play form (Battino, 2002) I was totally immersed in his life and writings. His system of logotherapy is designed to help clients find meaning in life. And, he uses paradox within that approach.

People who have no meaning in their life, no reason to exist and function and interact, are some of the most difficult to work with. Not only do they invariably see a glass as half empty, they feel isolated, abandoned, lost, loveless, helpless, and hopeless. What is there to live for? Suicide can be an out, yet in my studies in suicide it is almost always described as a permanent solution to a transient or temporary problem. There is a great emptiness or void in their lives—Where to? What next? Why? I am reminded of several poems by Omar Khayyám I memorized a long time ago:

> Into this Universe, and Why not knowing,
> Nor Whence, like Water willy-nilly flowing;
> And out of it, as Wind along the Waste,
> I know not Whither, willy-nilly blowing.

> Oh, threats of Hell and Hopes of Paradise!
> One thing at least is certain—This Life flies;
> One thing is certain and the rest is Lies;
> The Flower that once has blown forever dies.

> Strange, is it not? that of the myriads who
> Before us pass'd the door of Darkness through,
> Not one returns to tell us of the Road,
> Which to discover we must travel too.

> The Moving Finger writes; and, having writ,
> Moves on: nor all your Piety nor Wit
> Shall lure it back to cancel half a Line,
> Nor all your Tears wash out a Word of it.

These are eternal questions and need profound answers when exploring what is really important in life, and helping others find their way.

8.2 Life is With People

Sooner or later everyone I have spent time with who has had a life-challenging disease will say something to me like, "You know, Rubin, having this has been a blessing." This statement is confusing, paradoxical, and unexpected. A blessing? A New Zealand friend who had cancer of the prostate told me, "Until this happened I didn't know what love was, and I've been married to a woman I love for twenty-three years." How could this be?

Getting a diagnosis of a life-challenging disease like cancer frightens and isolates people, putting them into stasis and usually depression. (In our support group, sharing knowledge like this "normalizes" a person's experience and helps them cope.) Along with the sudden realization that their life is really finite (we all know this, but...), almost all of them begin to think about their remaining time and what is *really* important to them. All of a sudden that promotion, that book, that new car, that trip, that leak in the roof, that something they "had" to do, becomes less important, if not trivial. There is then the knowledge that relationships, people, are the single most important thing in their life. To love and be loved, to touch and be touched, to share, to care, to be with, to laugh and cry together, to just be together is the be-all and end-all. This is the source of meaning. One of the things that sustained Viktor Frankl throughout his time in the camps was thinking of his wife and holding conversations with her in his head.

A surprising thing that happens when someone is diagnosed with a life-challenging disease is that some friends and family suddenly become distant and remote. They do so for their own personal reasons. I share this with the people I work with and comment that the only thing they can do in such a situation is to be sad about the loss of that person in their lives, and move on. Speculating why gets nowhere. The saving and surprising thing that happens is that seemingly out of nowhere others enter their lives in meaningful ways. It may be a friend, a distant relative, a casual acquaintance, or someone like me who does this as his volunteer work. This is reality.

So, you reach out and others reach out to you. You cherish. You give and receive, and learn to ask for what you need knowing that you are *giving others* an opportunity to give. You call distant relatives and friends and work out ways to be with them. *Life is with people* and we need that nourishment. As Frankl said, "You always have choices" and the choices made when you are exploring what is really really really important in your life yield the meaning of what life is all about. Touch and you are touched. Love and you are loved. Be with and you are being with. Laugh and you are laughed with. Smile and you are smiled upon.

8.3 Life is With Nature

When people are searching for meaning in life they come up with relationships first and contact with Nature second. All of a sudden it becomes important to take a walk in the woods, enjoy thunder and thunderstorms and rain and snow, smell a flower, touch the bark of a tree, listen to the wind in treetops, be near moving water, whether it is a river or a stream, take in deeply the sounds and smells and colors and textures of Nature, and make contact with the earth that supports us. All of the patient rooms in Hospice of Dayton look out on sky and trees and bird feeders, and there are visiting geese from a nearby pond. We need that contact with our physical inheritance. There is the sun in the morning and the evening, and there are all of those stars and the moon at night. We are a part of, and apart from, the environment we live in. It is important to visit parks and zoos and lakes and oceans and mountains and nature preserves and just sit outside.

My Australian friend and colleague George W. Burns has written about the importance of contact with nature in doing therapy (Burns, 1998). He calls this "Nature-Guided Therapy" and finds that it is frequently helpful for him to guide his clients into making meaningful excursions into nature. There is something for the soul in having such experiences.

In August of 2011 my wife and I spent three weeks hiking in Glacier National Park and surrounding areas. What a renewal! Get out there and hike, stroll, wander, and wonder.

Life is with people and with Nature and that is what is really really really important.

Chapter Nine

Distance Writing, Structured Writing, and Workbooks

9.1 Introduction

There is something about keeping a journal or a diary and writing about your experiences and feelings that can be healing and therapeutic. In the 1800s and early 1900s many people kept diaries. I am the owner of the diaries of Bishop Wright, the father of the Wright Brothers. Not only did he make observations about his life and that of his family and events of the day, he also kept financial records. We have fallen out of that practice in favor of emails, phoning, texting, word-processor letters, and rare handwritten ones. The only writing I seem to do at the present time are the weekly postcards I send to my grandchildren (the children in the family with six kids get them every third week, and the children in the two-kid family every other week). We travel a fair amount and I have amassed enough scenic postcards to last me several years!

The three terms in the title of this chapter describe variations of the same approach, that is, writing that is done in response to a series of questions and in an organized manner. The questions are designed to help the writer solve a particular problem or deal with a specific condition. There is extensive literature in this field which was first developed by James Pennebaker (1997). A few references are:L'Abate, 1992; Esterling, et al., 1992; L'Abate, 1997; Pennebaker and Chung, 2007; L'Abate, 2007; Kacewicz, et al., 2007; and a "sourcebook" by L'Abate, 2011. The last book cited contains an enormous number of structured writing exercises designed for clients in mental health areas. L'Abate's website (http://www.mentalhealthhelp.com/) contains a great deal of information about this subject as well as many workbooks covering a huge range of topics. L'Abate feels that these workbooks will shorten the number of sessions that clients see therapists for, and will therefore be more efficient and more economical. He even feels that in the long run, distance or structured writing will have a powerful effect on face-to-face (f2f) talk therapy. Although he and I disagree on its long-range impact, this way of working with clients needs to be considered since it can be useful and impactful.

I reproduce in the next section a workbook I developed for helping people who have cancer so you can judge for yourself how the use of structured writing works. (Battino, 2000, pp. 214–217).

9.2 Workbook for People Who Have Cancer

The questions in this workbook have been designed to help you cope with a diagnosis of a life-challenging disease, and with its treatment. Please find a quiet time and place to do this writing over a period of successive days. What you write is personal and should be kept private. It is your decision about sharing any part of this, or all of it, with someone you trust. If you need more than the allotted space, please continue your responses on the back of the paper or on separate sheets. There are no "correct" responses—whatever you write is the right thing for you. Take whatever time you need to respond. You should know that a number of research studies have shown that the very act of writing responses to the kinds of questions in this workbook have been helpful in resolving painful concerns. [Note: space for writing responses has been deleted.]

1. Use the following space to respond to these three related questions. You may not be able to answer them with any certainty—in that case, a guess or a theory about how to answer the questions is fine.
    a. Why is this happening to me (versus someone else)?
    b. Why is this happening to me at this particular time of my life?
    c. Why do I have this particular kind of disease?

2. Do you know, or do you have a theory, or can you guess as to why at this particular time you are doing better, or worse, or staying the same?

3. What ways of taking care of yourself are you waiting to explore? (These can be things like second or third opinions, more research on available medical treatments, alternative or complementary treatments, support groups, support networks, or personal things like counseling/ psychotherapy.)

4. What is stopping you from exploring the options mentioned in 3 now? What resources do you need to be able to do whatever is necessary to help yourself with this?

5. Take some time to write about your fears for yourself, your family, and your future.

6. Take some time to write about your hopes and dreams, and what it is you would like to do with the remainder of your life. What are the things that you always wanted to do? Which of them can you do now? If your health improved, what are the things that you would be sure to do?

7. Write about your feelings about surgery, radiation, chemotherapy, or other treatments.

8. Some surgeries (like mastectomies and prostatectomies) involve the loss of body parts, particularly those that are related to body- and self-image. Please use this space to write about your feelings concerning these surgeries.

9. Write about your feelings about being in a hospital.

10. This question has to do with being able to communicate openly about your condition, and your feelings about this condition with the people in your life who care. Think carefully about who you can talk to about the following items, listing *specific* people in each row (for example, you may write in the name of a particular cousin in the row for relatives). For your guidance there are a number of general categories of people listed in the first column. In each box put a "+" if you would feel comfortable talking with them about that item, a "-" if this would be a mistake and they would be unresponsive, and a "?" if you are unsure of their responsiveness. Feel free to write additional comments in each box. Where there is more than one person in a category, like friends, please list them separately.

People	Physical Feelings	Emotional Feelings	Fears	Treatments	Information	Fun and Relaxation
Spouse						
Children						
Parents						
Relatives						
Friends						
Doctors						
Counselor						
God						
Minister						
People at Work						
Support Group						

11. Write about your feelings about dealing with medical personnel.
12. Write about what frustrates you about having this disease.

13. It is not unusual for people who have been diagnosed with a serious or life-challenging disease to have the seemingly paradoxical reaction of considering the disease to be a "blessing" in some way. What things have you learned about yourself and about the people around you that are beneficial to you?

14. How has having this disease changed your spiritual life?

15. Knowing what you know now about your life, if you could, how would you have lived differently? That is, what would you change about your past life?

16. Knowing what you know now about your life, what things will you do differently starting right now?

17. Sometimes opportunities for saying things to people just bypass us. Are there significant people in your past or in the present that you never had a chance to tell what was really on your mind? Write what you would have told them if you had the chance. (These people may be living or dead.)

18. This is related to 17. Write out what things for your spouse and children (or specific others) you want to: (a) have them know; (b) leave them (personal items or thoughts); and (c) say to them. You may wish to share these writings with them now, later, leave them for them, or continue to keep them private.

19. Although this is a trying time, it is always wise to take care of certain practical things like wills, living wills, durable power of attorney for health, financial matters, power of attorney, and funeral arrangements as soon as possible. Most people make these arrangements when they are well and not faced with difficult times. Once taken care of, you no longer need to be concerned about them. If you have not already done so, make appointments to take care of these items. This space would also be a good place to write about your feelings about these items. (Note: This item may be difficult to handle at this time, and you may wish to put it off for a while and/or discuss it with someone you trust. Please only respond to this item when you feel comfortable about doing so.)

20. Write about anything else that concerns you at this time. This is *your* private journal and you can write whatever you wish.

9.3 Concluding Comments

This chapter was included to give you some sense of a field of psychotherapy with which you may not be familiar. Giving clients homework assignments, particularly ones involving writing, can be useful. Aside from anything else the act of writing is a solo kinesthetic one which intimately connects the client with his/her feelings and ideas and possibilities. Depending on the circumstance this writing can be shared with the therapist or others or kept secret as was generally done in olden times.

Chapter Ten

The Importance of Family and Adopted Family

10.1 Commentary

An immediate family includes parents, siblings, and their spouses and children. An extended family includes all nephews and nieces, their significant others and their families, and many in-laws. I guess that you can reach further in terms of "blood" relatives. Once upon a time families and extended families lived within walking distance of each other, or a short distance away via some appropriate conveyance. In the modern world we are scattered all over our country, and even abroad. By and large we do not spend much "face time" with each other, and keep in touch via phone and email and, occasionally, written communications. All of these relatives have busy lives of their own which we touch from time to time, and on special occasions. Over time some family members get closer, others drift off into the ether, and it is not unusual for "grudges" based on old real or imaginary grievances to exist. We all know that Uncle X will not talk to Aunt Z and that Cousin Y has not communicated with her brother for twenty years. As the end of life nears for some of the older family members there are instances of reconciliation and even "death-bed" forgiveness and love. Aside from the complications of distance that exist now in many countries and cultures, not much has changed in this picture of families for millennia.

Given the modern family with contact at a distance, what fills the familial gap? For me this is my *adopted* family which consists of people I have "adopted" or who have done the same with me. These are obviously not formal legal adoptions. In the area where I live I have many sisters and brothers. To some I may be an uncle or grandfather. Occasionally, I am a surrogate parent (*in loco parentis*). The transition from friend to adopted family member can be swift or it can develop slowly over time until one day you know that Mary or Jim or George has become adopted family. My wife and I are members of the Yellow Springs Unitarian Universalist Fellowship and the members of this group are part of our adopted family, some closer than others, of course. Let me expand on this theme.

We have visited New Zealand seven times—for the first four times I was a visiting professor in chemical engineering at the University of Canterbury in Christchurch. The last three times we were tourists. We have four sets of close friends in Christchurch and have stayed at the homes of three of them for various lengths of time. We have hiked extensively with one of the couples and some with another couple. The men in these latter two couples are both chemical engineers and we have interacted professionally over the years, with my publishing with one of them. We got to be quite friendly with one of the couples because the husband and I shared an interest in the history of early flight. We spent much time with some people we met via friends in Yellow Springs—the two women had grown up together in London and then went separate ways. After the husband and wife had died in Christchurch I asked their daughter if I could "adopt" her daughter (our friends' granddaughter). So, in addition to our friends' daughter and husband I acquired another grandchild. I am in regular communication with these four families and they and we feel that we are related and have bonded as family. That is, I have four brothers and four sisters and one granddaughter in Christchurch. We do not see each other frequently, yet when we get together it is like only days have passed since the last time. This is what it is like with family—there are so many shared memories and feelings of closeness that time and distance disappear.

I have had two careers (psychotherapy and chemistry), am still active in both, and have "family" in both areas, in the U.S. and overseas. At the 11th Erickson Congress on hypnosis and psychotherapy in Phoenix, AZ, I was fortunate in being able to spend time with many of my brothers and sisters. One of my "brothers", who has spent much time immersed in Native American culture, always greets me as "Holy Brother." He and his wife and I spent a long evening together in conversation and with the joy of just being together. In the summer of 2009 I was at a chemistry conference in Colorado and slipped right into being with my chemistry family who were attending. A few years before that I met up with more of my overseas chemistry family at an international meeting in Boulder, CO. Again, our being together was natural and comfortable.

Closer to home there are a number of people where these familial bonds happen more frequently. These may be in weekly or monthly lunch meetings. We have an "old boys" group of retirees from the university who meet weekly for lunch, and have been doing so for thirty to forty years. And there are those friends with whom I communicate via an annual Christmas letter, sharing what has happened in our lives in the past twelve months. And they reciprocate. This is what families do—they keep in touch and share.

10.2 Some Suggestions

I have perhaps given too many examples about my adopted family—this was done deliberately to illustrate a variety of ways of adopting and being adopted. Family is everywhere if you are open to people. It is not unusual for bonds with adopted family members to be stronger and more meaningful than those with blood relations, and there is nothing wrong with that. You may wish to take some time now to think about the significant people in your life. Are there individuals, couples, families, or groups that you want to be part of, be closer to, to know better? Is there something that stops you from moving ahead on this? Of course, your overtures to get closer or to join may be rebuffed or unsuccessful. Yet, isn't the possibility of enriching your life in this way worth attempting? After some consideration, who will you phone or contact soon? Are there friends and relatives you were close to in the past or who you have lost touch with, that you would like to contact now? I am not into social media like Facebook (I have my own preferred contact methods), yet I am aware that they are a powerful way of keeping up and renewing relationships. Life is with people, and adopted family is something that has enriched my life—I hope it will enrich yours.

Chapter Eleven

Touch and Touching: A Dilemma?

11.1 Introduction

It is considered to be a no-no for psychotherapists to touch their clients. Perhaps the most frequent cause for losing a license is improper physical contact with a client. Medical professionals like doctors, nurses, physical therapists, medical technicians, and massage personnel have implicit permission to touch clients. Beyond shaking hands (even this is sometimes frowned upon!) other contact is considered to be unprofessional and forbidden. From my perspective this blanket proscription is unfortunate.

My volunteer work is with people who have life-challenging diseases, and also with caregivers. Effectively, I am working as a psychotherapist in this volunteer mode. When a person is in these stressed-out conditions they typically regress emotionally to childhood states. They want support and comfort and human interaction. Babies thrive on contact with their mothers and fathers. When being nursed or bottle-fed there is skin to skin contact, warmth, and sensations of heartbeats and breathing that are shared. Touching and being touched are essential. You might consider contact in this volunteer work to be permitted. If you do, then what is the difference in making physical contact (in an appropriate manner) with someone who is mentally distressed? The touching has to be of a different kind, and that is the subject of this chapter, but first let me mention several kinds of body work.

11.2 Body Work

There are many kinds of body work; the most common is thera-peutic massage. In the past I have experienced Rolfing (deep mus-cle work with the fascia), Trager, Alexander technique, Feldenkrais method, polarity therapy, yoga, craniosacral manipulation, osteo-pathic manipulation, Japanese acupressure, acupuncture, reflex-ology, physical therapy, lymphatic drainage, chiropractic, weight training, and I have even had my auras massaged. Aromatherapy may be included here, and there are many other ways. In Part II there is a chapter on bioenergetic analysis which is built on Wil-helm Reich's "body armor" ideas. They each have their own ratio-nale, philosophy, mystique and ways of working. Some approaches also use music with drumming and chanting. Dance and t'ai chi and martial arts can be included. A commonality would be that they all work with the muscles and joints and generally involve the practitioner touching and manipulating your body parts. Medita-tion is frequently part of the treatment.

The great variety of body work approaches and the large number of people who practice and experience these methods mean that their clients find the time and expense worthwhile. Many of these complementary methods are finding their way into hospital set-tings. The physical part of our lives cannot be ignored, and touch-ing and being touched is a central part of that.

11.3 Anchors

Within NLP the practice of setting and utilizing anchors is part of many of their procedures. An "anchor" is a reproducible stimulus that is connected with an idea or feeling or memory. Anchors are ubiquitous in our lives since another way of thinking about them is operant conditioning (from behavior modification). A particular stimulus evokes a consistent response, whether it be a bell that gets an animal to salivate or, for example, that look on the part of your spouse that invites you to romantic activity or tells you that you are in deep trouble. Anchors can be visual, auditory, kinesthetic, aro-matic or in tasting. The most powerful anchor appears to be odors, since the sense of smell is connected directly to a primitive part of the brain. If I asked you to think back to your childhood and inhale deeply, you would almost instantly be carried back to the kitchen of your childhood and aromas of good things baking. It is not unusual for a divorced person to respond to the perfume or a similar body odor of their ex-spouse. (I know that if I ever smelled the special fragrance that my first girlfriend used it would do strange things to me mentally and physically!)

Since you cannot avoid setting anchors when working with someone therapeutically (or in any interaction for that matter), it behooves you to be aware of the effects of anchors and to use them consciously. The V-K Dissociation technique that is used in NLP to treat phobias involves setting anchors for the phobia and for a comfort and resource state. As an example, this could be done by touching separate knuckles or different places on a shoulder. We can easily distinguish the pressure on two adjacent knuckles or two places on a shoulder separated by an inch or so. The touch is associated with a memory or an emotional state and the pressure is gently increased to "set" the anchor as you observe the client thinking and responding to the suggestion. By the amount of pressure you use on a given anchor you can adjust the extent of the memory or feeling. (These touches are generally soft.) An anchor can be tested by triggering it—touching it and observing changes in the person's physiology (breathing rate, muscle tension, etc.).

Anchors can be powerful so use them wisely.

11.4 Bonding

When you spend time with a client and they know you are listening to them, a bond or connection forms. With some clients I intentionally use bonding via hand-holding (with their permission) to establish a special kind of connection or bond. This is generally done during the hypnosis part of a session to reinforce or strengthen particular suggestions. With someone who has cancer, after making contact, I might say something like, "And now, through this contact with my hand, somehow, from me and through me, healing energy and knowledge is flowing from me to you. My immune system is intact and protecting me. You can just imagine that somehow from me and through me your own immune system is becoming more efficient, more effective, more powerful." With someone who has difficulty in being decisive, let's say, the words would be, "Through this contact you will be learning from me and through me how to know your own mind. In some interesting ways the patterns of thinking in your brain will become altered and adjusted so that you will know exactly what to do and how to do it as different circumstances arise. And this will be happening right now with new connections being made between neurons, some paths being bypassed and others strengthened, learning slowly and easily and naturally. Just one connection and change at a time. How surprised will you be as you gain knowledge and confidence? Yes and Yes and Yes. Thank you." (This is, of course, done with many pauses.)

"From me and through me" is the phraseology that is used since I do not know how these things occur, and I want the client to use her imagination to figure out just how this is happening, and to let it happen. The language is both specific and vague enough for the client to learn in her own way.

Some cautions about the way that you hold a hand. Sit close enough so that there is no awkward stretching. Get permission before doing this. Hold the client's hand *passively*, that is, without squeezing, just a gentle and comfortable contact. Occasionally, it is useful to suggest to the client that *they* can adjust the pressure of the contact depending on how much they need from and through you. This is good feedback.

Finally, remember that you cannot touch without being touched, or be touched without touching the other person. We all need to have "touching" experiences.

Chapter Twelve

Chuckling and Laughter and Having Fun

On one of my trips to South Africa, where my way was paid to do chemistry demonstration shows for school children, I had the good fortune of sharing a lecture with Doug Rivett, an experienced demonstrator. I learned three things from Doug about being an effective demonstrator. The first was that it was okay to be an openly eccentric lecturer in the English tradition of eccentricity. Students expect us to be a bit dotty anyway, so why not capitalize on it by dithering some? The second thing is that it is a requirement that the demonstrator openly and obviously enjoys doing the demonstrations. That is, if you are not having fun doing this, why should anyone be interested? The third is the importance of the well-placed chuckle. When you chuckle to yourself during a demonstration the audience is immediately alerted that something interesting is going to happen. Why else would that guy chuckle? The chuckle sets up an expectation of something different and unusual and fun. Chuckling can be overdone, and timing is everything.

I have found that the idea of chuckling can be quite effective in psychotherapy. When we can laugh at someone, something, or ourselves, it depotentiates the situation. Clients, in general, take themselves and their troubles very seriously, otherwise they would not be paying for therapy and investing the time. When you can get them to step back or outside of themselves and view their life situation from that external perspective and chuckle, light bulbs go off and a reframing occurs. They have been too close to see beyond the immediate circumstances. Their situation may be serious and dire and you will have to exercise good judgment to decide whether or not to introduce this distancing and a chuckle. It sometimes helps to relate a personal story about doing this with one of your own concerns.

A rationale I offer here is that human beings are imperfect and fallible and make mistakes and say things inadvertently without a sense of its impact. It is a great release for children at some time in their life (frequently in their thirties or forties) to look back and recognize that their parents were probably doing the best they could, but in their fallibility made mistakes. Again, when appropriate, the chuckle helps here. They may not do this immediately and may need time for this thought to make sense. The chuckle may have a place in your life and practice.

I once published an essay (Battino, 1973) entitled "If It Isn't Fun, What Is It?" for a chemical education journal. My thesis was that if you were not having fun teaching then you did not belong in the profession and your students would struggle to find interesting and useful things in your subject. When I taught freshman chemistry I would invariably do a chemistry fun and magic show for the first class session. In a Pavlovian way I wanted the students to associate that lecture hall and being with me as a good place to be. They all knew that chemistry is a difficult subject, and I never minced words about that (starting in the second lecture!). I also knew that many, if not most, of the students would soon forget the technical parts of the chemistry I taught, but they would remember the stories, the demonstrations, and the fun we had. In fact, my opening remark was, "I am here to have fun and enjoy myself. If you learn useful things, I will be pleased. If you do not, I will be a bit sad, and continue to enjoy myself."

So, does humor have a place in a psychotherapy session? I believe so, and there is frequently laughter in my consulting room. In amongst the serious stuff (which I take seriously) there is room for laughter. If this can be overdone, it can also be underdone. I once heard a tape by a well-known therapist telling about how when he worked in an agency he had to be careful because he heard from colleagues that there was too much laughter coming out of his office!

Milton Erickson was fond of puzzles and riddles and practical jokes. I believe that part of his intent in doing these things was simply to have fun and to depotentiate the "heaviness" that permeates many a therapy session. Telling an appropriate joke can not only lighten a session but also serve as a confusion technique: why is he/she telling me this now? What does it mean? What is its relevance to what we were just talking about? The client is then forced to go inside and search for connections. What is similar in my life to that of the protagonist or participants in the joke? Do we and our clients take things too seriously? A joke, laughter, chuckling, and a riddle all contain a distancing or dissociation from what can be an intense situation. In a sense, you might even consider that we and our clients are much too serious. Humor, of course, must be used with conscious intent and carefully, but it does have a place in a therapeutic session.

Let me end this chapter on a note describing the use of humor in the life-challenging support group which I facilitate. The people who attend can talk about whatever they wish while they are listened to attentively, yet somehow, despite these serious matters (or maybe because of them), we find much to laugh about together. This is not "gallows" humor; I believe it is the ability of human beings to show their inner strength and rise above the seeming constraints in their lives and conditions. In the midst of the travails we can all suffer, there is also space and time for joy. The musical *Fiddler on the Roof* is one example of this, and Viktor Frankl's observation that the inmates in concentration camps could enjoy a sunset or music is another.

A long time ago when I was an undergraduate student at The City College of the City of New York I was a member of the Laugh Society. Our motto was: "There is a crying need for laughter." So be it.

Chapter Thirteen

Inclusivity:
Either/Or vs. Both/And

Clients come to see us because they are stuck; that is, they know only one interpretation for a given stimulus in their life, and that interpretation leads to one response. Although this is a rather simplistic model of psychotherapy, it seems to fit the facts. This means that our main task as therapists is to help clients discover choices in interpretation and choices in responses. Then they are not stuck!

Also, both we and our clients tend to think about what is troubling them in an either/or fashion. They are depressed, panicked, anxious, obsessive, sad, grieving, unhappy, desperate, blocked, and limited OR they are not. Bill O'Hanlon (2003) found a fascinating way to deal with this stuck state of affairs. He calls it "inclusivity" which gets into the realm of both/and. This is an *oxymoronic* confusion or scrambled meaning technique. This is best illustrated by the following statements, generally prefaced by "I wonder how it would be or feel to be..."

happily depressed; depressedly happy
compulsively spontaneous; spontaneously compulsive
obsessively casual; casually obsessive
sadly delighted; delightedly or happily sad
desperately free; freely desperate
actively blocked; blocked actively
grievingly full of warm memories; warmly grieving
calmly panicked; panicked calmly
anxiously at peace; peacefully or calmly anxious
stressedly calm; calmly stressed

openly protective; protectively open
freely dependent; dependently free

Please note that these are all oxymorons, like a "down escalator" or "jumbo shrimp."

Recently, in the support group I facilitate, one of the members was talking about being depressed. This was first *normalized* by another group member talking about how depressed she had been, and is still occasionally depressed about having cancer. I pointed out that almost everyone I know who has been diagnosed with a life-challenging disease goes through depression at one time or another. Then I said, "I wonder what it would be like to be happily depressed." The confusion that appeared in his face was a wonder to behold. Others in the group got the idea and added many both/and comments. (I leave this to your imagination.) He began to smile with the novelty of these new ideas. How could he be depressedly alive and active? What would it be like to be energetically slothful?

Inclusive statements scramble thinking and provide interesting choices to what had hitherto been restricted. I hope that the more you think about the transformation involved in going from either/or to both/and will provide you with choices in your own life and also choices for your clients. You might even become effectively ineffective, for example.

Chapter Fourteen

Eye Movement Approaches

14.1 Introduction

The eyes have been spoken of as "the windows to the soul." They can be much more. Medical doctors and ophthalmologists can tell a great deal about your health from examining your eyes, and this is always a part of their routine examinations. There are people who are "shifty eyed" and those who look at you directly or seductively or sadly or encouragingly, etc. We instinctively look at the eyes of people we interact with for clues about them. As therapists can we utilize the way that people look at us, the way we look at them, and eye movements? In this chapter I am going to briefly explore three eye-related areas: (1) NLP's eye accessing cues; (2) Eye Movement Desensitization and Reprocessing (EMDR); and (3) Eye Movement Integration (EMI).

14.2 Eye Accessing Cues

For most people the direction in which they move their eyes when thinking or speaking in the auditory, visual, or kinesthetic mode appears to be the same. There is some controversy in the literature about this, but you can easily calibrate it for the person you are observing. This can be done by either asking questions that would require accessing information in one of these three modes, or listening to them and observing their eyes when they use one of these modes. The figure on page 74 is for right-hand/left-brain speaking individuals, and is oriented for you looking *at them*. When a person looks up and to the left they are accessing stored internal mental images or pictures. When looking up to the right they are *constructing* a mental image or picture. Looking straight left is for accessing internal auditory messages, and looking straight right is for constructing sounds. A down and right look is for kinesthetic states from memory or current time, and down left is for talking to yourself. Some people may show the reverse pattern.

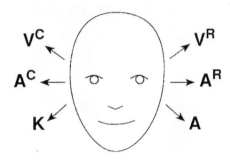

There are two practical things that you can do with eye accessing cues. The first is that it is useful to know what your client's internal states are, and what they are feeling or doing mentally while they are talking to you. Are they listening to a voice from the past, talking to themselves, looking at old images from the past or creating new ones, or are they accessing kinesthetic feelings? You can almost seem like a mind reader when you ask, "What are you hearing now?" There is an NLP procedure called "Strategies" in which it is possible to track the sequence of mental steps a person goes through; for example, when they make a decision or motivate themselves. You can practice this when you are in a group, with another person, or watching a movie or TV. Is there a correspondence between where the speaker looks and what she says? If eye accessing cues make sense to you, please use them.

14.3 Eye Movement Desensitization and Reprocessing (EMDR)

EMDR is a proprietary psychotherapy which was developed by Francine Shapiro, Ph.D. (Shapiro, 2002; Maxfield, et al., 2007). The technique was developed to resolve the development of trauma related disorders caused by exposure to distressing, traumatizing, or negative life events. When a traumatic or distressing experience occurs, according to Shapiro it may overwhelm a person's usual cognitive and neurological coping mechanisms. This means that memory and the associated stimuli of the event are inadequately processed and then dysfunctionally stored in an isolated memory network. EMDR therapy is then used to process these distressing memories, reduce their lingering influence, and allow clients to develop more adaptive coping mechanisms. In fact, EMDR was developed for post-traumatic stress disorder (PTSD).

In the process of psychotherapy using EMDR the client recalls a traumatic event while simultaneously undergoing bilateral stimulation that can consist of moving the eyes from side to side, tapping movements or vibrations on different sides of the body, or tones delivered through one ear and then the other via headphones. There is an eight-phase structured approach that addresses the past, present, and future aspects of the traumatic or distressing memory that has been dysfunctionally stored.

There is a fair amount of evidence that this works, but be aware that you do need to have the special training given for this proprietary form of therapy.

14.4 Eye Movement Integration

Eye Movement Integration (EMI) was developed by the NLP practitioners Connirae and Steve Andreas in 1989 to treat traumatic memories. The best known practitioner and trainer is Danie Beaulieu, Ph.D. and her book (Beaulieu, 2003) is the primer on the subject. Beaulieu uses a broad definition of trauma which she defines as "any experience that leaves an imprint that continues to give rise to negative effects and recurrences in one or more of the sensory, emotional, or cognitive systems." The approach is based on the principle that eye movements that are naturally associated with accessing sensory, cognitive and affective information can be guided externally to facilitate the integration of traumatic memories.

In its present form EMI consists of identifying a disturbing memory which is the apparent precipitating or underlying cause for the client's current distress, and then facilitating activation and integration of that memory with other multisensory information by a guided series of eye movement patterns. The patterns or figures cover the entire visual field of the client, and this is intended as an aid in accessing the full spectrum of information processing modes internally available to the client. As the client holds the memory in consciousness, each eye movement pattern is executed with the client, following the guiding movement of the therapist's hand. Then, during a pause between each figure and the succeeding one, alterations in the client's internal representation of the memory are assessed. This allows the client to explore changes in sensory and physical modalities and new associations which arise with the facilitated process. This specifically excludes extensive discussion or commentary from the therapist. Integration is considered to be complete when eye movements in *all* regions of the visual field elicit only positive information in the various sensory modes, and the client is no longer distressed when recalling the memory.

I happen to believe, and this is a subjective judgment, that EMI has more potential to be successful with PTSD clients than EMDR. Of course, like EMDR it requires much training and experience. My judgment is based in part on EMI using the entire visual field in establishing integration. Both of these eye movement approaches can be a useful part of what you do with appropriate training. Perhaps, "The eyes have it!"

Chapter Fifteen

Cognitive Hypnotherapy and the Three Gifts

15.1 Introduction

Trevor Silvester, a friend and colleague from the UK, is the founder of The Quest Institute which he runs with his wife Rebecca. He has written three books (Silvester, 2003; Silvester, 2006; Silvester, 2010). The blurb for the first *Wordweaving* book states:

> *Wordweaving* presents a radical new approach to the use of hypnotic suggestion. For years hypnotherapists have used scripts which are aimed at a particular problem, like smoking or weight loss, rather than aiming at the client who smokes or has weight issues. This book suggests that it is not the problem that is the problem; it's the client's unique relationship with the problem that's the problem. Mastering this book will free you from the constraints of scripts and enable you to use your creative skill to weave subtle spells that empower your clients by changing their model of reality. It presents the science behind suggestion, and the means of using that science to create magical ways of influencing others.

The blurb on the second *Wordweaving* book states in part:

> In *The Question is the Answer* Trevor Silvester shows you how to ask the questions that provide you with the information you need to create hypnotic language patterns

specifically for each client, and guide them to finding their own answers to life's problems.

And lastly, here is a useful blurb from the *Cognitive Hypnotherapy* book:

> *Cognitive Hypnotherapy* is a model that can be used to create a unique treatment plan for each client, using techniques drawn from any school of thought, and integrated into a single model that uses the client's own mind to solve their own problems.

These blurbs promise a great deal, and in my opinion the author is successful at delivering those promises. The most recent book is chock-full of useful ideas and suggestions. In the next section I am only going to give details about one of them: Three Gifts.

15.2 *Three Gifts*

With respect to this exercise, Silvester indicates (2010, pp. 229–231) that positive psychologists have found that over a seven-day period their approach was more effective in raising the mood of people with depression than Prozac (Seligman, M.E.P., 2003). The exercise is quite simple and the directions are as follows:

> Each evening for one week look back over your day and select three positive things that have happened and write them down. Also, please write down how you were responsible for those "gifts" occurring.

The ability to find three "gifts" each day tends to grow as the week moves on since the client will be looking for them. This is obviously a solution-focused exercise that can be considered to be based on an "As-If" modality. It is also strongly connected to Pennebaker's exercise (Pennebaker, 1997; Pennebaker and Chung, 2007) of simply having students (and others, of course) writing for twenty minutes daily for two weeks about their emotions. The magic of this exercise is in the developing *expectation* of the person of finding gifts in their daily lives. Also, writing about how they were *responsible* for the occurrence of these gifts is empowering and an important part of the instructions.

The Three Gifts idea is easily expanded into the following:

Gratitude—Find three opportunities in any given day to thank somebody for something beyond the run of every-day pleasantries.

Savoring—Set aside a period of time every day for savoring. Choose two or three things each day. These can be bites of food, Nature, family members, or anything you interact with. Immerse yourself fully in the pleasure of it.

Kindness—Do an act of *random* kindness every day. Do this without any thought of personal gain, and also do it at some cost or inconvenience to you if possible.

Are you in growth or protection?—When faced with a life choice or business decision, ask yourself, "Which decision keeps me in growth?" "Am I in growth or protection?" "Where is that decision coming from?"

These are all rather easy activities, but they can have profound effects on how you feel about yourself. You may wish to practice this yourself, and you may also wish to introduce the "three gifts" idea as presented above to others in appropriate settings. There is much more in Silvester's books.

Chapter Sixteen

Transforming Negative Self-Talk

16.1 Introduction

Steve Andreas recently published a book (Andreas, 2012) on how to transform negative self-talk. The book contains many practical exercises and some great illustrations of this kind of work. I recall that one of the important parts of Transactional Analysis was concerned with dealing with what they described as "Witch Messages." These were negative messages given to us (usually when we were young) by significant people in our lives. These negative messages were primarily of the type that limited behavior and self-image and the possibilities in our future lives. Some examples follow:

> You're bad, just bad.
> You'll never succeed.
> Why are you such a negative/mean/unloving/inconsiderate/helpless/sad/miserable/stupid/ignorant/disobedient/rebellious/ugly/impossible/uncaring/selfish/self-centered/ornery child?
> How can you be so unfeeling?
> You'll never find someone who would marry you.
> You just never learn, do you?
> Why can't you be like your (sibling) who does everything right?
> God will punish you for this, you'll see.
> You'll never get to heaven.

The remarkable thing about human beings, especially when they are young, is how impressionable and receptive they are to these pretty horrific messages. If one of these messages is given to a child over and over again (as they usually are), it is then no wonder that they will believe the message given to them by such a powerful and important person, and that they will incorporate the message as one of their core beliefs about themselves. This belief is not to be questioned, and must be followed and lived out. After a while the message is just part of the person and they may not even consciously say it to themselves, yet it is there and controls their behavior and their life.

The sad thing about these messages is that the intent of the giver is almost always benevolent in the sense that they feel they are correcting their child and giving them good advice about how to function in the world. These messages are frequently considered to be of the same ilk as "look both ways before you cross the street," and "don't take things from people you do not know," and "be sure to dress warm," and "always be respectful to older people." There are genuinely malicious people, but mostly these "witch" messages are given unknowingly in good faith.

People who are fortunate simply outgrow the witch messages based on their life experiences. They do succeed, they do find someone to love and who loves them, they do learn how to feel emotions, and they do end up feeling good about themselves. However, many of the people who seek out therapists exhibit the restrictions on their lives and feelings and behaviors that were injected into them when they were younger. This negative self-talk is usually quite obvious to an experienced therapist, who may ask, "What are you saying to yourself when you do that?" or "Who told you that?" or "What is going through your mind now?" Andreas's book has many helpful exercises and ideas for counteracting negative messages. In the next section I will present a few useful things from Andreas's book (2012) which I recommend you buy and study.

16.2 Andreas Exercises and Change Processes

To give you the scope of Andreas's book, I list below the eleven chapter headings. There is also an extensive introduction.

1. Changing Location
2. Changing Tempo and Locality

3. Adding Music or a Song
4. Talking to Yourself Positively
5. Adding a Voice
6. Auditory Perspective
7. Starting Your Day
8. Generalizations, Evaluations, Presuppositions, and Deletions
9. Negative messages and Positive Outcomes
10. Asking Questions
11. Transforming a Message

Since much of what Andreas is doing with negative self-talk has to do with changing the submodalities of such talk, it would be helpful to discuss submodalities briefly. A "modality" in NLP terms is a sense like auditory, visual or kinesthetic. You can change the visual modality by altering its size, shape, proximity, intensity, or color, for example. In a similar way an auditory modality can be altered by changing its volume, location, tempo, or tonality. In the NLP "Swish" technique, guiding a client to change her self-image from a negative or restricting one to a positive or expanding one is done by utilizing appropriate changes in submodalities. In the following subsections several of Andreas's approaches will be described in sufficient detail to whet your interest in his work, and enable you to use some of it immediately.

A. Changing Location

First identify the location of the troublesome voice. Is it somewhere inside your head or is it somewhere outside? If it is outside, is it in front, behind, to one side or another, above or below? And, if it is outside, is it pointed toward you or away from you or somewhere in between, with toward you being the most common direction? Experiment with changing the location of the outside voice, i.e. near or far, left or right, up or down. Notice what happens when you hear the outside voice from a different location. Then, listen to that voice when it comes from the location that is the least disturbing.

You can change the location of the troublesome voice inside your body. Notice what happens when you let it come from a big toe, your kneecap, your heart, an elbow or an index finger. Return the voice to the original internal location. Which was the most troubling?

With the voice coming from outside your body, hear it when it is ten, twenty, thirty, and one hundred feet away from you. What happens then? Change the location and distance to in front, behind, and to your left and right. Just notice what happens when you allow the voice to move to these different locations. Realize that you can change the location, and that changing the location becomes easier with practice.

The self-critical voice may start its statement with "I am…" or "You are…" This is an important distinction to notice. Notice what happens when you change "I am…" to "You are…" Whose voice is making the statement? Is it yours or someone else's? Does an image come with the speaker? If it does, change the image of the speaker to a more comfortable location.

Change the volume of the voice by either moving it farther away or turning down an imagined volume control. What happens then? Notice that when you rehearse these changes they become more and more a part of your automatic thinking.

Andreas has an important warning (2012, p. 23): "You can try any experiment briefly for the purpose of learning, but when you make a change that feels worse, it is very important to respect that, and change the voice back to what it was like before the experiment, and try something else." He also notes (pp. 23–24), "The overall goal of this book is to teach you how to transform a troublesome voice into something much more useful and supportive, but not to eliminate it." That is, you can "talk" with the voice and find out its intent, and then decide how to exist with it or remove it.

B. Adding Music or a Song

Here, I will just quote the mood shift exercise on p. 44 to give you a sense of one of the many exercises in the book.

> Think of a problem mood that you slip into repeatedly and would like to have more choice about…
>
> Now think of some music that might possibly be useful to pair with this mood, and then hear this music in your mind…
>
> As you continue to hear the music, think of a time when you felt this problem mood strongly, and notice what happens…

Then try doing this with a different piece of music, and another…until you find one that shifts your mood in a useful way…

Then think of when and where this music is likely to be useful to you in the future…and then imagine being in that situation…and hear the music in your head in order to offer more choice.

C. Talking to Yourself Positively

Many self-help books and proponents push the idea of saying positive things to yourself. In a way this is an example of acting in the "As-If" mode. I had a client not too long ago who told me that she had recently decided to be happy. That decision changed her way of being in the world. Notice what happens when you say the following sentence to yourself with one of the variants in the sentence, "What else can I enjoy/learn/appreciate/love/see more clearly/understand/try right now?" The word "else" is an important component of this sentence as it implies and presupposes that you are already doing one of those things.

Andreas (p. 52) was working with a client who was depressed. He gave his client the following suggestions:

"…look around and mentally say to herself, 'I am sitting on this happy chair. There is this happy table. And there are those happy windows with happy curtains.' I made her do this for about ten minutes. I suggested she do this every day for about ten or fifteen minutes."

The client did this and recovered from her depression. What happened? She was noticing happy *things* and this implied to her that *she* was happy! This works best with inanimate objects rather than people or animals. Other adjectives like peaceful or calm or loving or comfortable or balanced can be substituted for happy.

To end this section here are some instructions from Andreas's (p. 55) "appreciate and smile" exercise:

With their eyes closed, I ask clients to imagine they are standing in front of the front door to their home. I ask them to feel the key in their hands and hear it turning in the lock as they open the door. And then I ask them to appreciate the door, and smile…Then I ask them to go around the home and appreciate and smile at everything they see or hear…

And then repeat the same process of appreciating and smiling with all the family members, neighbors, and acquaintances.

And then do the same for the other places that they visit often, like office, school, or shops.

And then repeat this with some other strangers as well…

And I also ask them to go inside their own bodies and appreciate and smile with all their body parts…

The exercise takes about fifteen minutes to teach, and people take about the same amount of time to do it on their own. This is quite simple, and another example of the As-If change process.

Continuing the As-If way of changing behavior, Andreas quotes Nardone and Portelli (2005, p. 73) with the following set of instructions which appear to be a variant of the Miracle Question:

During the following weeks, I'd like you to ask yourself this question. Every day, in the morning, question yourself: "What would I do differently today if I no longer had my problem, or if I had recovered from my problem?" Among all the things that come to your mind, choose the smallest, most minimal but concrete thing, and put it into practice. Every day, choose a small but concrete thing as if you had already overcome your problem, and voluntarily put it into practice. Every day choose something different.

Significant words in this set of instructions are "smallest" and "concrete." The other essential part of the instructions is "put it into practice" which is the acting As-If component.

D. Transforming a Message

This clever and practical method of transforming a message was developed by Melanie Davis, a therapist in the UK, and is the core of the last chapter in Andreas's book. In essence it is a wonderful way of reframing negative self-talk, as you will discover in what follows. The elements of the method are described by Andreas (pp. 109–110):

1. Presuppose that what your client has been saying to himself is positive and useful, but has been badly misunderstood.
2. Divide the sentence into two or more parts.
3. Use auditory ambiguity to find a different meaning in the same sounds (or similar sounds) that is more positive, enjoyable, humorous, or even nonsensical.
4. Use a different intonation and inflection that is cheerful, playful, and humorous, instead of the serious or unpleasant one in the original statement.
5. The meaning of the message is changed, but no attempt is made to change the intensity of the client's feeling response.

Here are some examples of Davis's work (CL = client; MD = Davis):

CL: I'm no good.
MD: Say "I am."
CL: I am.
MD: Yes, you are. Say "I know good."
CL: I know good.
MD: Yes, you do, and I think it is more of a command, something you are supposed to do. So, what good do you know?
(CL started listing the good things she knew and the group helped by expanding on this.)
CL: I'm useless.
MD: Keep saying "I am."
CL: I am. (MD then kept telling him, "Yes, you are.)
MD: (In a command tone) Use less! Use less! Use less! (CL started laughing.)
CL: Don't think I will sleep tonight.
MD: (wrote down "don't think" and then said) Breathe in and then wonder what it would be like to not think. (CL smiled.) And, when you don't think, what do you think will happen?
(CL smiled really broadly and responded "I will sleep tonight." And she did!)

Clients tend to make declarative statements, like a few examples below taken from Andreas's workshop exercises (pp. 111–113). The first statement is what the client might say, and the second statement(s) in quotes contain possible responses by the therapist that his workshop attendees offered.

1. I'll never be able to sleep. "I'll never! Be able to sleep." "I will? Never! Be able!...to sleep."
2. I can't sleep. "I can! T'sleep." "Eye can?" "I can knot! Sleep." "I can't? Sleep."
3. Something's wrong with me. "Something is...Row with me." "Some thin sarong with me." "Some think strong with me."
4. It's not fair. "It is! Not fair?" "It's a nut fair." "It's a knot a fair." (Last with an Italian accent!)
5. No one likes me. "No! ONE likes me." "Know: one likes me!"

Recall that for all of these rewordings and changes of emphases that you may have to write out or spell the new words or phrases. Obviously, Melanie Davis has an exceptionally clever way with words, and you can have fun practicing with your own statements of "can't" and "never" and "not", and with those of your clients.

16.3 Some Concluding Observations

At this time in my life I am not aware of any negative self-talk, probably having grown out of it. I know that when I was younger there were negative thoughts about being socially adept, being attractive to women, not being lovable, and not really being competent as a scientist to name a few. So, what happened to that negative self-talk? I am now in my ninth decade of life and have had many experiences and been through my own therapy, albeit many years ago. I do not recall coming across anything in Andreas's book about negative self-talk that diminishes with time and experience, and then just vanishes. As we grow older, most of us (I hope!) learn from experiences that challenge these old negations. I am socially comfortable, I found love, and I have a solid reputation both as a scientist and as a therapist. What I am writing is that if you are open to the reality around you, then that reality can negate that negative self-talk.

One way of helping people access the realities in their lives is to get them to do a life review. The very process of doing this via writing an autobiography provides much validation of a life well spent and full of various accomplishments. For a number of years I have videotaped friends and relatives and people from my volunteer work who have life-challenging diseases talking about their lives. The DVDs are made available to them and their families. In my experience, although some people are reluctant to do these interviews and invariably tell me that they have very little to talk about, typically they easily fill up two hours and have learned much in the process of telling their personal histories. On the other hand, no matter what your age, if you still hear and tell yourself negative things, then you may find a release in this chapter or from a therapist who knows how to use the material herein.

Chapter Seventeen

On the Importance of Non-Importance—The "Nonesuch"

In the wonderful musical *Big River* there is a scene which involves a carnival that Huck and Jim go to. A huckster is getting people to see a sideshow about the Nonesuch. In those days sideshows had "freaks" in them who were tiny or huge or super obese or super strong or had bizarre bodies. The Nonesuch was billed as one of the most remarkable of these people, or "creatures" as they were sometimes referred to. I do not know the inspiration of the name Nonesuch, yet it has echoes in me of many things. The Nonesuch is out of the ordinary. It is an example of there being nothing like it existing in the world. How can there be something such of which there is none or nothing? We are confusedly in the world of paradox. Yet, the world of psychotherapy is confusing and full of paradoxes. This is so much so that in hypnosis we have the "confusion technique" and there has been much written about the uses of paradox, including Viktor Frankl's paradoxical intention. How do we deal with confusion and paradox and the emptiness of Nonesuch? Is the Nonesuch the unseen elephant in the room which somehow fills all of the space? How do you work with what is not there? And is it important?

Clients can fill a therapeutic hour with endless information. How do you filter out the important stuff? In my Gestalt Therapy training we were told to not worry about this and just pick anything the client says and go with that. It seems that all client statements eventually lead to gold or can be developed into useful material. Is doing this a shortcut or will it stretch out the therapy? How many roads can you travel down? (Is this the marvel of Robert Frost's poem "The Road Not Taken"?) Is the life and experiences of the client sitting in your office full of unimportant trivia *and* meaningful trivia? Can unimportant things be raised to or actually made part of what is really really really important in that person's life? Wow! We are getting inextricably enmeshed in philosophical puzzles. What to do?

Listen and observe and ye shall be enlightened. Marvel at life's complexities, and the simplicity of some solutions. I like doing the work I do since I find people to be endlessly interesting. They are infinitely unique and yet they do get stuck in many similar ways. We can dream of being like Milton Erickson, of whom it was said that he invented a new therapy for each client. (Is this time for another "wow"? Insoo Kim Berg's interjection of a "wow" at an appropriate time set the standard in this area for moving a client along. We wonder at the Wow! and the Nonesuch. And wondering embodies the awe needed to be able to really really really be in the same space and place and time as your client.

A search on the internet for "nonesuch" found a dictionary definition of "a person or thing without equal." Interesting. I also found the lyrics for the Nonesuch song. The singer describes the Nonesuch as having one big breast in the middle or her chest, and an eye in the middle of her nose! Such a description would certainly intrigue the men (and possibly the women) in small towns along the Mississippi

The ever-present difficulty in a therapy session of the client saying something and you not knowing what to say or do next can be bypassed by following a set of procedures in which you have been trained. For practitioners of NLP it is the Meta Model, wherein you listen carefully to the client's words from a linguistic perspective, and let that decide your response. For example, if the client uses a nominalization, then that is challenged. Others may reflect the client's statement back to them and empathize. Some may automatically reframe, or ask questions for clarification. As I mentioned above, in my Gestalt Therapy training we were taught to follow up on *any* statement, assuming that all self-descriptions (that's what they are) will lead to useful changes. In a way, this is an application of Milton Erickson's utilization principle, i.e. build on and extend whatever the client brings into your office. When a client brings in a complaint, a Gestalt Therapy approach is to exaggerate the difficulty or complaint, and to escalate the complaint ("and then what happens?") until it leads to absurdity or exhaustion or insight. This is entering into the client's world and staying with her until new possibilities and choices appear. In his minimalist approach, Ernest L. Rossi has the client go inside with his concerns and then guides him with "A bit more of that," or "Just let that move inside you to a new place," or "Yes. Good," or "And, then..." The client knows you are with him. He is not alone as he explores his inner world.

I was fascinated by the barker's description of the Nonesuch. The essence to me of being a therapist is in the definition of the None-such as "a person or thing without equal." When you consider your client to be *without equal*, and she knows this, then whatever you say or do will be impactful. You accept her as she is, and possibilities for change will arise from your conversation (chatting), and via the experiments in thinking and doing that you share with her.

Part II
Alternative Approaches to Therapy

Introduction to Part II

In my workshops that include segments involving older approaches to psychotherapy I have noticed that a significant number of attendees do not know anything about these older approaches. Part II is quite selective from my viewpoint since there are well over 500 named ways of doing therapy. I can only write about the older approaches I have been trained in that I find to still be useful in my judgment and in my practice. I recently finished reading Kottler and Carlson's book on their finest hour (Kottler and Carlson, 2011), which contains chapters of many of the best therapists they know talking about special cases. I was surprised to find that in my hubris that I was familiar with the work of only a handful of these super therapists. This is mentioned here to give you some perspective on what follows in this idiosyncratic section. Reading Kottler and Carlson's book was humbling. In their final summarizing chapter (with Myf Maple) Carlson wrote (pp. 373–374):

> The single common factor that stood out to me (as well as to Jeffrey Kottler) was that each expert loves people. They value the human experience and were able to find hope and possibility for the hopeless and impossible. They were able to create relationships of safety in which clients could take risks and become like the *Man of la Mancha* and "dream the impossible dream." It really stood out to me that the contributors felt that people mattered to them much more than things or even ideas. They consistently supported and attended to their clients, and less so the facts or presenting (often overwhelming) problems. They saw their roles as freeing the client to become what the

client wanted and not trying to be gods or goddesses to shape others' futures.

This is something to strive for, for ourselves. Perhaps, in a small way, the material in Part II will help.

Chapter Eighteen

Behavior Modification

In a sense we can consider all psychotherapy as being behavior modification. At a number of conferences where I watched demonstrations with volunteers I found it interesting to speculate if what the "super" therapist was demonstrating (regardless of his or her stated or known approach to therapy) could have been described as behavior modification. After all, clients come to us because they are stuck in some particular behavior pattern that they find unproductive or uncomfortable or disturbing. From this perspective our job is to somehow influence them to change their behavior. So, what we are doing *is* behavior modification. Yet this term does not seem to be used any longer. It is more in vogue nowadays to attempt to connect changes in behavior to one kind of brain scan, or one kind of gene transformation, or one kind of biochemical or another. Perhaps it is that simply changing behavior is too simple! One of Milton Erickson's teachings was to get the client to do *one* thing differently. That frequently opened the door for a cascade of other changes.

Operant conditioning and behavior modification began with Pavlov's experiments, continued to those of B. F. Skinner, and developed further with people like John Watson of the University of Chicago. Watson was widely quoted as stating, "Give me the child and I can cause him to develop in the direction I would choose." There was a strong belief that behavior could be changed with conditioning. Not much is said about this anymore, except for those who still use conditioning for treating phobias via systematic desensitization, where a stimulus that causes anxiety is paired with a pleasant one. In aversive conditioning unwanted habits are paired with unpleasant stimuli.

Currently Cognitive Behavioral Therapy (CBT) is considered by many to be the approach of choice since there is a large literature showing that it works with a variety of mental health diagnoses. The definitive current book is the one by Judith Beck and her father, Aaron T. Beck, the founder of CBT (Beck and Beck, 2011). Their description of CBT (www.beckinstitute.org) is:

> Developed by Dr. Aaron T. Beck, Cognitive Therapy (CT), or Cognitive Behavior Therapy (CBT), is a form of psychotherapy in which the therapist and client work together to identify and solve problems. Therapists use the Cognitive Model to help clients overcome their difficulties by changing their thinking, behavior, and emotional responses. Cognitive therapy has been found to be effective in more than 1000 outcome studies for a myriad of psychiatric disorders, including depression, anxiety disorders, eating disorders, and substance abuse, among others, and it is currently being tested for personality disorders. It has also been demonstrated to be effective as an adjunctive treatment to medication for serious mental disorders such as bipolar disorder and schizophrenia. Cognitive therapy has been extended to and studied for adolescents and children, couples, and families. Its efficacy has also been established in the treatment of certain medical disorders, such as irritable bowel syndrome, chronic fatigue syndrome, hypertension, fibromyalgia, post-myocardial infarction depression, non-cardiac chest pain, cancer, diabetes, migraine, and other chronic pain disorders.

I must admit that I have some difficulty with approaches that have been "manualized," since that seems to me to be too rigid when working with real people. Yet there have been many studies (as cited above) showing that CBT works well with many clients.

Dialectical Behavior Therapy (DBT) was first developed by Marsha M. Linehan (1993). A current book (Koerner and Linehan, 2012) provides a practical guide to this approach. A DBT training group (www.dbttherapy.com) gives the following description of this approach:

> Dialectical Behavior Therapy (DBT) is a skill-building therapeutic approach developed in the 1970s by Marsha Linehan, Ph.D. Although DBT was originally developed

for the treatment of women with Borderline Personality Disorder (BPD), it has proven effective for a wide range of psychiatric disorders, including depression, anxiety disorders, substance abuse, and eating disorders. [...] DBT is an evidence-based treatment modality, meaning it has been heavily researched in numerous clinical trials. Research shows that through DBT therapy and DBT skills groups, you can learn healthy coping skills that can help you make a lasting recovery from your psychiatric disorder. [...] Dialectical Behavior Therapy involves three main components: individual DBT therapy sessions, DBT skills groups, and phone coaching.

This is obviously a powerful and impressive approach for working with rather difficult clients. DBT apparently involves many components which must be carried out in specific ways. This appears to me to be too complicated. Plus, I am always a bit suspicious of approaches that have numbered steps that must be followed. On the other hand, I take my hat off to people who can devise these methods and applaud their successes in using them. Much can be learned from CBT and DBT.

"Behavior Mod" is currently alive in ways that would probably not be recognizable to the people who originated it. So be it.

Chapter Nineteen

Gestalt Therapy

19.1 Introduction

My first training experience was in Gestalt Therapy in the first program offered by the Gestalt Therapy Institute of Southwestern Ohio. The trainers were Howard H. Fink, Ph.D., and Bob Timms, Ph.D. Fink had started his experiences and training with Fritz Perls when Perls had begun his travels around the U.S. doing demonstrations and training. Fink met Perls in Columbus, Ohio; my training was in Dayton. The training was a fascinating learning experience for me for several reasons. When I was at the City College of New York I was primarily interested in creative writing and psychotherapy. Having grown up in the Depression I had no idea as to how I would be able to earn a living in those areas. However, I had the advantage of two years of chemistry at the Bronx High School of Science before beginning college. At the time it was apparent to me that it would be much easier getting ahead and earning a living in chemistry (which I enjoyed) than in the other two fields. Then, in my mid-forties the opportunity opened up to begin a second career in psychotherapy. Fink must have had a great deal of confidence in me since I was the only person in his initial training group who did not have an advanced degree in counseling or psychology (one of the members was a psychiatrist). I was surprised to find that I could hold my own with all of these professionals.

Training in Gestalt Therapy in those days (and probably today) was essentially done in the old guild master/apprentice manner. That is, we held weekly group meetings in which individuals worked with one of the trainers. (Later, we all had the experience of working with each other in this group setting.) One of the group members would ask a question or talk about something that was troubling them. They then became the focus of one of the trainers and the group. This person was in the hot seat. Sometimes the trainer would explain and expand on what he was doing. Other times it was a matter of observe and learn. There were also many group exercises. This was the era of "encounter groups", with their many ways of involving people in learning experiences. (During this time I also attended a variety of encounter groups run by "traveling" therapists.) Thus, the training was by total immersion in experiences in the group.

When I had been seeing Fink in individual sessions as my therapist, I was also involved in a therapy group he ran. A memorable, fascinating and tiring experience I had when in treatment with Fink was a 24-hour marathon with three therapists and a dozen group members. (In Chapter 22 I will write more about group therapy.)

Let me cite here two of the seminal books in this area: Perls (1969) and Polster and Polster (1973). Also of interest are two more recent books: Polster, 1987; and Mann, 2010. The latter includes 100 key points and techniques in Gestalt Therapy.

19.2 Group Work and Psychotherapy Groups

I know that group work is currently being used in many settings, particularly institutional ones like prisons, HMOs, local service agencies, drug and alcohol rehabilitation programs, schools, and incidentally in the support group I facilitate for people with life-challenging diseases and caregivers. In the 60s and 70s it was common for a therapist to run one or more groups along with his/her private practice. There were regional and national conferences on group therapy. At a recent international conference on Ericksonian work I attended I do not recall any sessions that were specifically oriented towards group work. I did attend one workshop with only eight participants that turned out to be primarily about group work, and thoroughly enjoyed being in that milieu again. Are groups too hard to organize in private practices? Is managed care reimbursement getting in the way? Or are there fewer therapists trained in and experienced in using group therapy? I do not know the answers to these questions. My experiences with group work suggested that they were effective. We live and function in many different kinds of groups, from family to work to recreation to religion. It just makes sense to me to do more group work since it can be considered to be more efficient in that more than one person is involved in each session.

Group psychotherapy started in the U.S. in the first half of the twentieth century. Irvin Yalom was a major contributor to the field and the 5th edition of his *The Theory and Practice of Group Psychotherapy* (Yalom and Leszcz, 2005) is the standard work in the field. There are some common therapeutic factors which are cited in this book, and they are: universality, altruism, instillation of hope, imparting information, corrective recapitulation of the primary family experience, development of socializing techniques, imitative behavior, cohesiveness, existential factors, catharsis, interpersonal learning, and self-understanding.

The primary organization in the U.S. on group psychotherapy is the American Group Psychotherapy Association (www.agpa.org). On their website, under the heading Group Works! and the subheading of Evidence for the Effectiveness of Group Therapy, they state:

> During the last thirty years, studies have shown the growing benefits of group psychotherapy in a number of areas of life challenge. Through groups, individuals find a forum of peer support, gaining strength as they share their feelings and experiences with others who are facing the same obstacles themselves. Some gain strength in seeing the resourcefulness of those in the same situation, while others renew their feelings of self-worth through assisting others.

They then list some of the kinds of groups which are helpful: addictions and substance abuse, cancer patients, HIV/AIDS patients, character disorders, depression and grief, eating disorders, and youth violence. AGPA holds regional and annual meetings, has regional chapters, and their website can be consulted for meeting dates.

19.3 Language and Gestalt Therapy

Once a group member is in the hot seat he is the focus of the group's attention. He now has the opportunity to interact with others and to have the group witness whatever is going on. We

live with people, and in a group we can participate actively or passively with each other. (Isn't passive interaction still interaction?)
Of course, it is essential that everyone knows that what is said in
the group is *confidential* and is to stay in the session and the group.

When a person talks about what concerns them there are many
openings for intervention and follow-up. Some avenues may be more
productive to explore than others. Gestalt therapists consider that
you can choose any segment of an opening statement by the client
about what is bothering or troubling them, and productively build
on that. This has been my experience. A person may state that they
panic in certain situations. Staying with that they may be directed to
experience the panic more strongly and notice what happens. Then
they are asked to experience it even more strongly. This *exaggeration*
of a symptom continues until the symptom becomes absurd or incon-
sequential since the person just cannot conceive of anything worse.
Staying with the symptom as it gets stronger to its illogical (or logical!) conclusion helps erase it and put it into a perspective that makes
it ho-hum and ordinary. Exaggeration generally works.

The group can be used to listen to a statement by the person on
the hot seat by having her make it individually to each group member separately, making eye contact (or staring off into the distance),
and perhaps saying:

I hate my mother. [Whoever.]

I am anxious right now. [There are many emotions.]

I just do not know what to do with my life.

Sometimes I feel like I am going crazy.

I am afraid of dying. [There are many fears.]

No! No! No! [and, Yes! Yes! Yes!]

My boss is an asshole. [many such!]

I'll never get better. [There are endless "never" statements.]

No one ever loved me.

Why? Why? Why?

It takes courage to make these statements. Depending on the
statement the group members are instructed to remain passive or

nod their heads or make some useful response. The very act of saying out loud what you have been secretly thinking and harboring is
freeing. Going around a circle like this can be emotional for everyone. Having an audience roots the experience in reality.

One of my favorite linguistic responses to hearing a litany of
woes is "So?" This is generally accompanied by a shrug. "So?" can
be repeated as many times as necessary as a part of exaggeration
and also to depotentiate the unchanging state of what the person
has been complaining about. It questions the generally exagger-
ated importance of the trouble/concern/problem and helps put it
in perspective. It is a kind of reframing. (Note that the use of "So?"
can be overdone.)

19.4 Two-Chairs

Perhaps the two-chair approach is the best known of the Gestalt
Therapy techniques. It is suggested to the client that it would be useful in resolving a current or old conflict with others or within himself to have a conversation with the participating components which
may be real or imaginary, and can also be objects. Examples are:

- Unfinished business with a living or dead person of significance.
- Finding a way to continue the relationship with someone
  who has died, instead of attaining closure. (Robert A. Neimeyer states, "Closure is for bank accounts, not for love accounts. Those remain open.")
- Polarities within the person, such as feeling up/feeling
  down; calm/anxious/panicked; right/wrong; love/hate;
  sad/happy; and good/bad.

A frequent use of two-chairs is unfinished business with a dead
parent. There were things you wished to say to your parent that
never got said. You may not have been on speaking terms with
them, they may have died before you had a chance to say goodbye,
or it may be that you simply never had the courage to tell them
what was on your mind and that has festered within you. It is suggested to the client that now is the time to take care of this. The
client can do this between the chair they are sitting in and another
empty chair facing it. I find it better to use two other chairs so that

where they were sitting can serve as an external observation post. "So, your mother is over there in that chair. Please tell her what is on your mind." [The therapist guides this conversation, suggests things to say, and tells the client when to switch to the other chair.] "Now, how would your mother respond to what you just told her?" Mother responds. The conversation between the two continues until a resolution is achieved. This may take half a dozen or more exchanges, and it is amazing that the unfinished business is resolved in that short time. It is also amazing that as the client changes chairs his affect and voice quality change accordingly. Also, it is my observation that when being immersed in the two-chair experience the client is invariably in a trance state. They usually get so engrossed in each persona that the experience takes on a dreamlike characteristic. In another sense the two-chair experience can be considered to be a mini psychodrama (see Chapter 25).

To illustrate the good/bad polarity, you can suggest that your bad part is over there and you are now your good part. Talk to each other. Neimeyer makes the significant point that in grieving for a dead relative just completing unfinished business or attaining closure can be an incomplete part of the discussion. Deceased loved ones continue to be with us forever in terms of memories and feelings. In this sense, two-chairs can be a way to retain the loving feelings that have now been expressed, and then move on.

19.5 Commentary

Gestalt Therapy via individual or group work has its place. My good friend, colleague and trainer, Howard H. Fink, Ph.D., was eclectic and studied many different ways of doing therapy. Since he was so good at using Gestalt Therapy it made sense for him to primarily work in that modality. Although I write about many ways of working in this book, I, too, have a preferred modality, which is "chatting" accompanied by hypnosis. However, every once in a while, other ways of working creep in!

Chapter Twenty

Bioenergetic Analysis

20.1 Origins

The origins of Bioenergetic Analysis as formulated by Alexander Lowen are in the work of the controversial psychiatrist Wilhelm Reich (he was actually jailed for promoting the "orgone box" as a method of healing in a more conservative and less enlightened era). Reich had the idea that there is a memory in the body in its muscles and bones and organs, something he called "character armor." When we learn particular ways of protecting ourselves in our youth this gets locked into our musculature with things like tight muscles, frozen smiles, rigid postures, and hunched shoulders. In the latter, a person actually hunkers down between their shoulders for protection. The goal of many of the approaches mentioned in the body work chapter is to free or loosen up these rigid and tight body contractions and formations. There are memories locked into the physiology of our bodies in the way that we hold ourselves and our postures.

20.2 Bioenergetic Analysis

Bioenergetic Analysis was developed, promulgated and taught by Alexander Lowen (1958, 1975). It involves body work as well as analysis, as Lowen came out of a psychoanalytic background. I went through several years of training in this work, and the training sessions were all in groups where we were taught what to look for and what to do, actively participated in the exercises, and were "worked on" ourselves. I never ended up using bioenergetics in my private practice and I suspect that my fellow trainees did not either. Doing hands-on things was not something you did in institutional settings, and you had to be very careful about it in private practice. Nevertheless, the approach can be quite an effective and powerful change agent. It would be safe to say that all of the trainees benefitted from the training in personal ways; I know I did.

The two central themes in bioenergetic work are breathing and grounding. One of the most successful exercises had to do with a breathing stool (bending over it) and working with breathing. There are people who hold their breath a great deal, others who breathe shallowly, some deeply, etc. We learned to recognize breathing patterns and how to help a person breathe in ways that released locked-in emotions. Just as emotions can be locked into muscles and bodily postures, they can also be locked into breathing patterns. The next time you are with a group of people or in a setting where you can observe their breathing patterns, take note of all of the variations you can observe. One of the rapport building skills of pacing and leading has to do with matching a person's breathing pattern. In bioenergetics the goal is to do things that will release "holding" patterns to free up what has been frozen in, due to whatever reasons.

Grounding has to do with our relationship to the ground, Mother Earth and terra firma. Do you make contact? Can you feel support? What are the arches like? Are the knees flexed or locked? Are you grounded or floating? Do you "have your feet on the ground" or are you "up in the air"? If appropriate, then some analysis can help the client to understand and move on.

There are five character types that are connected to the five types of holding which we were taught to identify:

Holding Together	Schizoid	existence vs. need
Holding On	Oral	need vs. independence
Holding Up	Psychopathic	independence vs. closeness
Holding In	Masochistic	closeness vs. freedom
Holding Back	Rigid	freedom vs. surrender to love

These character types made sense within the context of the training. Nowadays they appear to be anachronistic!

Obviously, touching is used in bioenergetics in different ways than discussed in the chapter on the importance of touching (Chapter 11). I included this short segment on bioenergetics because it had a profound effect on my life at one time, and some readers may find the subject interesting enough to pursue further. Finally, there were two guiding principles:

YOU ARE YOUR BODY
THE BODY NEVER LIES

Chapter Twenty-One

Neurolinguistic Programming (NLP)

21.1 Introduction

When Richard Bandler and John Grinder introduced NLP via their first two books on "the structure of magic" (Bandler and Grinder, 1975; Grinder and Bandler, 1976), they started a minor revolution in how therapy was done. Bandler had some experience with Gestalt Therapy and was a computer programmer. Grinder was an academic who specialized in linguistics. They were fascinated by the seeming "magic" of three exceptional therapists: Fritz Perls, Virginia Satir, and Milton H. Erickson. These three appeared to be more effective than other therapists. In particular, Bandler and Grinder analyzed their use of language from the perspective of linguistics to find out if this analysis would identify useful patterns that could be taught. What was different in the way these three used language? How did their use of language get clients unstuck? The basic question they asked was, "When the client says something, how do you know what to say next?"

21.2 The Meta Model of Language

Much of what Grinder and Bandler described in language usage was based on Noam Chomsky's *transformational grammar*. Most statements are *surface structure*; that is, they only contain a limited portion of what the person wishes to convey. The example I use most frequently is, "Jo(e) hurt me." I ask a class to listen to this statement, close their eyes, and decide what the statement means. Then I ask a few questions: (1) Is Jo(e) male or female? (2) Is the "hurt" physical or mental? (3) Is the "hurt" strong or mild? (4) Who is "me" in the sense of what mental image they have of the "me" person (old, young, married, single, child, etc.)? The test sentence is missing a great deal of detail, and the class generally fills in those details based on *their* own backgrounds and *their* hypotheses of what they think is going on in this interaction. The sentence is incomplete in terms of conveying information.

A *deep structure* statement is one which contains as complete information as is linguistically possible. An approximation of such a statement might be, "My husband Joe hurt me by slapping me hard across the face." This statement describes the action and the relationship. These are words which put the message in context and provide "color" and history to the statement, since there is a deeper level which involves the person's memories and feelings. With sufficient questioning we may be able to obtain from the client a more complete sense of her interpretations and reactions. In some circumstances it may be important to dig into this deeper level. That would be a judgment call.

The Meta Model has many ways of going from the surface to the deep structure of a communication, and this is basically the content of the two structure of magic books. This means that there is a great deal to learn about language and language forms and this is one aspect of training in NLP. I should point out here that the longest chapter in *Ericksonian Approaches*, and which I wrote (Battino and South, 2005, pp. 65–144), is on language usage in hypnosis, and is mainly based on the linguistic contributions made by Bandler and Grinder and their colleagues.

Before writing a bit about the Meta Model I copy here a list of NLP *presuppositions* that I used when I taught an introductory course on NLP in 1995:

> The map is not the territory. We all have different maps of the world. No map reflects the world completely and accurately.
> Mind and body are part of the same cybernetic system. Mind and body affect each other.
> The meaning of the communication is the response it elicits.
> Resistance is a comment about the communicator.

If what you are doing isn't working, do anything else.

People make the best possible choices with the information they have.

The element with the most flexibility will be the most controlling in the system.

Behind every behavior is a positive intention.

There is no failure, only feedback. If something doesn't work, you can utilize that feedback and try anything else.

If one person can learn to do something, anyone else can.

People work perfectly. No one is broken.

Every behavior is useful in some context.

Choice is better than no choice.

People have within them all the resources they need.

Anything can be accomplished if the task is taken in enough small chunks.

This list of presuppositions is full of hope and practical advice and is a guide for all practicing therapists. Bits and pieces of it are strewn throughout this book, and it is good to have it in one place. These are the goals of the Meta Model:

- To find out what is going on now.
- What do you want? What is the desired outcome?
- What stops your client from getting this right now?
- Find out what your client needs to get over what is preventing him/her from going from their present state to their desired state.
- How would the client know if they got there? (The desired state must be testable in *sensory experience*.)

Rather than reproduce all of the goodies in the Meta Model I am just going to present a few parts that I particularly like and use, and urge you to study the two books on the structure of magic, the two books which analyze Milton Erickson's use of language (Bandler and Grinder, 1975; Grinder, DeLozier and Bandler, 1977), recent books on NLP and the classics in the field. (Crown House Publishing is a good source for books on NLP.)

Here are a few examples of language usage that are particularly useful:

Deletions—portions of the deep structure are missing in the surface structure; e.g. "I am angry."

Nominalizations—basically converting a verb to a noun. Diagnoses are the most common form of this (like depression or anxiety) which are challenged by something like, "How are you depressing yourself?" The latter converts the noun back into a verb.

Presuppositions—something must be implicitly assumed to understand what has been said; e.g. "No one loves me." "Why aren't you paying any attention to me?"

Modal Operators of Necessity—something *must* occur or *cannot* occur; e.g. "I can't relax." "I shouldn't let anyone touch me." "I must work harder."

Universal Quantifiers—these are generalizations: all, each, every, any, nobody, anyone, etc. For example, "She never listens to me." "I'm always uncomfortable around authority."

Complex Equivalence—two statements which are equivalent in the person's model of the world; often a causal connection is implied. For example, "She's always yelling at me...she hates me." "He acts different...he must be crazy."

Cause–Effect—a link is made between an external stimulus and an internal event even when the two are not directly connected; e.g. "This _____ makes be bored." "I wish you wouldn't make me so nervous."

Mind Reading—the belief that one person can know what another is thinking or feeling, but without direct communication; e.g. "When he looks at me like that I know just what he is thinking." "She doesn't understand the need for discipline."

Meta Question—"How do you feel about feeling _____ ?" A good question to ask.

The Meta Model when used on its own can frequently help in moving a session along. It certainly bears studying and learning.

21.3 Three Quotes From My Notes

History is a set of lies agreed upon.
Napoleon Bonaparte

History repeats itself; that's one of the things that's wrong with history.
Clarence Darrow

The cat having sat upon a hot stove lid, will not sit upon the hot stove lid again. Nor upon a cold stove lid.
Mark Twain

21.4 Brief Description of Some NLP Techniques

A. Changing Personal History

Personal histories are sets of perceptions about past experiences and as such can be altered. That is, memory is malleable. The abbreviated steps follow:

1. Identify the present concern context, i.e. the setting of the difficulty.
2. Isolate the kinesthetic (K) component and anchor it so that it can be accessible.
3. Holding the K anchor, have the client do an internal search to find the first time they had the K reaction or the response or the behavior they wish to change.
4. Access or develop a present-day resource (or capability) to help in the past. Anchor this present-day resource (several resources are better).
5. Trigger the resource (from the present), and then the past via K. Hold *both* until you get a positive indication that the process is working.
6. Satisfaction check—"How do you know you feel good?" That is, experience the past in a positive way.
7. Future pace—Imagine the experience, but without the anchors. Can the client change in the future? If necessary, anchor a trigger to recall the resource in future situations. This trigger can be a natural movement like holding two fingers together or scratching behind the ear.

B. Seven-Step Reframing

This can be used for psychosomatic problems and unwanted behaviors or responses. (It is different from content or context reframing.) These are the steps:

1. Identify the pattern (X) to be changed.
2. Establish communication with the part that is responsible for the pattern. "Will the part of me that runs X communicate with me in consciousness?" Establish a yes/no signal like a finger movement or a head nod.
3. Distinguish between the *behavior* of pattern X and the *intention* of the internal part that is responsible for the behavior. "Would you be willing to let me know in consciousness what you are trying to do for me with pattern X?" If "yes" then ask that the intention be communicated. Is that intention acceptable to consciousness? If "no" reassure that part that its intention and help in the past is appreciated, and that it may wish to communicate the reason(s) in the future.
4. At the *unconscious level* have the part that runs X communicate its intention to the creative part so that it can select at least three realistic alternatives generated by the creative part. When each alternative is selected have the "yes" signal given.
5. Ask the part running X, "Are you willing to run the new alternatives in the appropriate context?"
6. Ecological check—"Is there any part of me that objects to the new alternatives?" If "yes" recycle back to Step 4 and repeat until there are no objections.
7. Future pace—Think of a time when you would have normally X-ed. Know that you now have choices. (This may be made available by triggering an anchor for this.)

C. V-K Dissociation for Phobias

This process works on phobias and traumatic life situations. The "real" history or the associations cannot be changed, but the kinesthetic responses can be diminished and even extinguished. Phobics react to a visual stimulus (usually the primary one) with a visual internal stimulus which triggers a kinesthetic response. The V-K dissociation process works to break the V-K link. It tends to work very well with people who have clear-cut phobias with a point of origin (real or imaginary), and where there is no secondary gain. Phobias need respect and have realistic components, i.e. some snakes are dangerous and walking near the edge of some heights can also be dangerous—this needs to be mentioned. Since a phobia is typically learned quickly from one instance, it means that phobics are fast learners and the phobia can be extinguished quickly. The steps for the process follow:

1. Pick a code name, color, symbol, or letter for the phobia.
2. Establish a powerful anchor in the present for comfort, safety, maturity, and resourcefulness. Two or three positive resources in the present can be anchored.
3. Holding the resource anchor(s) have the person visualize himself out in the very first scene of the traumatic incident, making it a "still-shot." The client sees his younger self before him. Details should be visualized too. It helps here to ask the person to imagine himself sitting in a movie theater seeing that first incident up on the screen.
4. When he can visualize this still-shot clearly, have him float out of his body (as if to the projection booth) so that he can see himself sitting there watching his younger self on the screen. Anchor this three-place dissociation.
5. Now have the person out front run the traumatic experience through to the end while maintaining the anchors for present-day resources and the dissociations. Use appropriate language to emphasize these resources and separations.
6. The movie can be run forward in black and white, and then very rapidly run backward in color to the time before the incident occurred.
7. When the experience has been completely *seen*, have the third person (observer) float back into the second place (here and now).
8. Next, have the present-day person (still anchored to the therapist and present-day resources) go to their younger self and reassure him that he is from his future, and that the younger self will never have to go through this experience again. That is, the younger self is given the support and appreciation for having gone through this experience.
9. When the present-day person can see that his younger self understands, have him integrate by reaching out and bring-

ing his younger self back inside his body. He is now part of you. With the energy freed from the old phobic response have the unconscious mind pick some particularly pleasurable activity that this unbound energy can be used for.

10. Check that the process has worked by triggering the phobia and observing the person's response. Future-pace so that the person can continue to function phobia-free.

This is an elaborate procedure which I have used many times to help clients over phobias. The process usually takes 20–25 minutes. (Some NLP practitioners use variations of the above.)

D. Submodalities and the Swish

Submodalities are smaller elements within each modality. They are literally the ways in which our brains sort and code our experience. Words are only inadequate labels for our experience. For example, within the visual modality are the submodalities of color, distance, depth, clarity, contrast, scope, movement, speed, hue, transparency, aspect ratio, orientation, and the foreground/background relationship. Within the Swish approach are the following steps:

1. *Identify Context*—Where are you broken or stuck? Where or when would you like to behave or respond differently than you do now?

2. *Identify Cue Picture*—Identify what you actually see in that situation just *before* you start the behavior you don't like. See this cue picture *associated* (this means going back and reliving the experience), i.e. be in it seeing what you see there.

3. *Create Outcome Picture*—Create a second image of how you would like to see yourself differently, as if you had already accomplished the desired change. Keep adjusting this image until you have one that is really attractive to you. See this outcome picture *dissociated*, i.e. looking at the memory image from any point of view *other* than from your own eyes.

4. *Swish*—Now "swish" these two pictures. Start with seeing that cue picture big and bright. Then, put a small dark image of the outcome picture in the lower right-hand corner. The small dark image will grow big and bright and cover the first cue picture, which will get dim and dark

and shrink away just as fast as you can say "swish." Then blank out the screen (or open your eyes). Swish it again a total of five times, getting faster each time. Be sure to blank out the screen at the end of each swish.

5. *Test*—Now picture that first image. What happens? Or, you can provide them with the cue or stimulus and observe how they respond.

Note that this pattern is *generative* in that it creates a direction for behavior. Brains learn very fast. Sometimes it is useful to first "calibrate" how a client adjusts the submodalities to change how they experience an event or feeling or behavior. This is done by having them make an image of something that is mildly unpleasant, and then changing the submodalities and noticing how they change their reactions to this mildly unpleasant image. By calibrating first you can tailor the way that the cue and outcome images are seen and modified and replaced.

E. Other NLP Approaches

As I indicated earlier, NLP practitioners have been quite creative in adapting and inventing ways of working within the NLP framework. For example, there is a two-volume "encyclopedia" (Bodenhamer and Hall, 2001; Hall and Bodenhamer, 2003) that describes almost endless ways of working in this field. One of the most interesting of the NLP approaches is called Time Line Therapy and it was developed by James and Woodsmall (1988). It is a variant of changing personal history that has a person travel back on their time line and make adjustments to what happened back then; then, after returning to the present, they "look" forward at how this will have changed their future. I still make use of many NLP ideas from time to time. Three good sources within the U.S. are:

www.nlpco.com (NLP Comprehensive)

www.realpeoplepress.com/blog/ (Steve Andreas's blog)

www.steveandreas.com

Chapter Twenty-Two

Encounter Groups and Group Therapy

22.1 Encounter Groups

When I first started exploring possibilities for myself in the psychotherapy world it was during the era of encounter groups. There were groups based on all kinds of premises, from primal scream to Gestalt Therapy to expanding human awareness. Two books you can read are *Joy: 20 Years Later* (Schutz, 1989), and *Awareness: Exploring, Experimenting, Experiencing* (Stevens, J. O. (Andreas, Steve), 2007). Both books are chock-full of things to do to expand awareness. Let me begin with paraphrasing a review of this book in Amazon.com (full review connected to the book) by reviewer William Bagley. He indicated that he had read this book in college, and that the exercises were both open-ended and simple. Further, the exercises help people to explore and learn from their own inner psychology. Doing the exercises, which are presented as scripts, can heal and also expand awareness. Many of the exercises are designed for groups. Bagley also liked the non-judgmental nature of the exercises, and the way they allowed making personally useful discoveries on your own.

A few quotes from Stevens's introduction tell more:

> This book is about awareness, and how you can explore, expand and deepen your awareness. Most of the book consists of experiments which ask you to focus your awareness in certain directions to see what you can discover. It's incredible how much you can realize about

your experience by simply paying close attention to it and becoming more deeply aware of your own experiencing. What the sages have said for centuries is really true: the world is right here—all we have to do is empty our "minds" and open ourselves to receive it. (p. 1)

This book is based on the discovery that it is much more useful to simply become deeply aware of yourself as you are now. Rather than try to change, stop, or avoid something that you don't like in yourself, it is much more effective to stay with it and become more deeply aware of it. You can't improve on your own functioning; you can only interfere with it, distort it, and disguise it. When you really get in touch with your own experiencing, you will find that change takes place by itself, without your effort or planning. With full awareness you can let happen whatever wants to happen, with confidence that it will work out well. You can learn to let go and live and flow with your experiencing and happening instead of frustrating yourself with demands to be different. All the energy that is locked up in the battle between trying to change and resisting change can become available for participation in the happening of your life that is both passive and active. This approach will not provide you with answers to the problems of your life. It does provide you with tools you can use to explore your life, simplify and clarify your problems and confusions, and help you discover *your* answers—what you want to do. (pp. 2–3)

In the chapter on interpersonal relations in Schutz's book (1989), two exercises are presented here to give you an idea of what these are like.

MILLING

Leader says, "I would like you to get up, one at a time, and walk toward me and keep walking in any direction you want. Stop wherever you feel most comfortable. Don't try to figure out where you want to be. Just let your body lead you to where it wants to go. If you don't feel like settling, keep milling around. When others come near, you may feel like turning, moving away, moving toward them, or staying still. Do what you feel. We will just continue milling until everyone is located somewhere, or is constantly moving."

The group leader also follows these instructions. When the group members have completed this task, they sit down and discuss the experience. (p. 95)

THE ENCOUNTER

You and I are asked to stand at opposite ends of the room. We are instructed to remain silent, look into each other's eyes, and walk very slowly toward each other. Without planning anything, when we get close to each other, we are to do whatever we feel impelled to do. We continue the encounter for as long as we wish. After it is completed, we talk about our feelings, and others will contribute their observations and identifications. It works best if we let our feelings take over and do not plan what we will do when we meet. (p. 99)

One of the givens in these encounter groups is the "processing" that occurs after an exercise, although there are some exercises which forbid processing afterwards. There is a great deal of sharing of ideas and feelings. When you participate in such a group you have entered a special community of people who all become relatives. These experiences can be so powerful and the relationships so important that the leaders spend time at the end of a group talking about the "re-entry" problem. That is, how do you go back to "normal" life with family, significant others, and colleagues in your workplace? This reaction can happen in religious retreats, work retreats, and in any special group. Returning home from spending time with "the boys" or "the girls" or at an interest group can involve re-entry concerns.

Although the heyday of encounter groups is long past, there are so many things they pioneered that can be useful in all kinds of social and group settings today that it makes sense to me to resurrect much of what they taught us about social interactions. I must admit that I miss them!

22.2 Therapy Groups

Since there are different kinds of therapy and support groups, let me begin here with the way that being in a group can help someone. My mother-in-law Ellie was as independent as can be. She died a few months shy of turning 94. About forty years earlier she divorced her husband and used her sewing skills honed by courses at the Fashion Institute of Technology in New York City to establish a new life for herself. After she retired at 65 she moved to Yellow Springs, where we live and set up house. Here she got into sports, which was something she had always wanted to do but was really not available to her when growing up in Gettysburg, PA. Ellie learned how to swim and also became involved in the Senior Olympics, eventually settling on the field sports of javelin, discus, and shot put. She competed in all of the national Senior Olympics meets until her last one in Louisville, KY, where at 91 she won a gold medal (javelin) and two bronze medals. She had a major abdominal operation, from which she recovered and went back to single living; however, it became evident that she could no longer live independently so we helped her move to the assisted living facility in town (with lots of grumbling, of course!). Ellie came back to life there. We attributed this to her living with other people, having prepared meals three times each day at a table for four, going on outings, and being involved in activities that she enjoyed, such as bingo and Trivial Pursuit. Her meds were controlled by the staff. Living in a group and being with other people when she wanted to made the difference. To repeat an earlier statement, *life is with people*. I do not think she realized how isolated she had become with her independent lifestyle, particularly when it became restricted by physical problems. It was wonderful that in the year before her death we were able to take her on a trip to Gettysburg to attend her 75th high school reunion (she was the oldest person there and the only one from her class). Also in that year we took her to Youngstown, OH, where she was inducted into the Ohio Senior Olympics Hall of Fame (incidentally, her great granddaughter Ellie attended this event as a surprise!).

Aside from the pride I have in telling this story of Ellie, the significance here is that we need and thrive with the interaction with other people. This is especially the case with people who get stuck in such ways in their lives that they find it useful and helpful to visit a therapist. As good as we may be in one-on-one and face-to-face therapy, we are leaving out the social context within which people live. Family therapists who involve not only immediate family, but also extended family, are taking care of this. Narrative Therapy (Chapter 27) has one of its strengths in involving the family and the community. Short of such involvement, group therapy in its many manifestations fills the gap.

There are many different kinds of support groups. To name a few: Alcoholics Anonymous, Weight Watchers, diabetes, Parkinson's disease, Alzheimer's disease, smoking, narcotics, cancer, and caregivers. Almost every major disease has a support group. Some are primarily informational and others provide emotional support. And there are special interest and hobby groups, from stamps to quilting to religious to reading to ethnic to woodworking to singles to sports to crafts to art to square-dancing to… Many of these groups have their own magazines and local, regional, and national meetings. People need people, and shared interests and passions are universal evidence of this. In the remainder of this chapter I am going to briefly present some information about the support group I facilitate, and a specific purpose one used by Rachel Naomi Remen.

22.3 The Charlie Brown Exceptional Patient and Caregiver Support Group of Yellow Springs

This group was started in 1990 by a man named Charlie Flynn who was a hospice patient. He had read Bernie Siegel's book, *Love, Medicine and Miracles* (1986, 1990) and it provided him with so much hope that he "graduated" from the hospice and lived for another three years before dying of a heart attack on Christmas Eve. With two hospice nurses and a clinical psychologist they started an ECaP (Exceptional Cancer Patient) group. This group followed ECaP principles, but also had an AA flavor since Charlie had been a member at one time. They met at Hospice of Dayton, although there was no formal connection between the two groups. After reading Bernie's book I tracked down this local group and they let me attend. Eventually I became the facilitator, the group moved to the Yellow Springs Senior Center, and formally included caregivers.

The group is free and is open to anyone who would like to attend. It meets twice each month for ninety minutes, all year round. After conducting any business and giving follow-ups on members who could not attend, the group's operating guidelines are presented if there is a new member. Otherwise, we proceed to going around the circle where each member can say what he/she wishes to, and the rest of us *listen attentively*, without making any comments or asking any questions. We operate under rules of confidentiality and what is said during a meeting stays there. After everyone has spoken there is a short period of time for making comments or adding things. The group ends with everyone sitting in a circle, holding hands, and the facilitator does a closing healing meditation for a few minutes. We have found that being able to say whatever you wish and knowing that you are being listened to is healing. We have a small lending library of books and recordings, and everyone has a name tag.

Even though I am a licensed professional clinical counselor, I do not function in that capacity within the group. We heal each other by the act of active silent listening in this caring and sharing community. There can be laughter and weeping. We enjoy being together.

I occasionally do individual volunteer work with people (whether they are members or not), and this may involve therapy. It also generally involves healing guided imagery work which results in a guided imagery recording.

22.4 Remen's Healing Preparation Circle

Rachel Naomi Remen, M.D., (1996, pp. 151–153) under the heading of "Making Caring Visible," describes a ritual to help a person get through an invasive medical intervention like chemotherapy, surgery, or radiation. The day before the procedure the person gets together with close friends and family. Before the meeting the central person is asked to find a small, flat, ordinary stone and a piece of the earth that can easily fit into the palm of their hand. This group sits in a circle and can speak in any order. A group member is given the stone, and tells a story of a time when they faced a life crisis. As part of the story they reflect on the personal quality that they felt helped them live through that difficult time. Then they will say something like, "I put love in this stone for you," or "I put inner strength in this stone for you," or "What brought me through was humor," or "It was my faith." The characteristic that helped them through their crisis is put into the stone. Before it is time for the procedure in the hospital the stone is taped to a foot or a hand or some place out of the way. The person then goes through the procedure armed with and protected by all of the characteristics that were embedded in the stone by their loved ones. Remen comments (1996, p. 153), "Ritual is one of the oldest ways to mobilize the power of community for healing. It makes the caring of the community visible, tangible, real."

I would like to expand on this in two ways. First, I prefer to describe this healing circle as a *ceremony* rather than a ritual. To me a ceremony has something of the *sacred* connected to it, whereas a ritual is more like a habit, something that is repeated. Marriage is a ceremony, brushing your teeth is a ritual. Second, I believe this kind of ceremony can be expanded and generalized to include any kind of difficult activity that frightens or immobilizes a person, such as speaking before an audience, taking an exam, breaking a habit, leaving for a trip, or starting or terminating a relationship. The sacred healing and protective object can be a piece of jewelry or a card on which is written the gift characteristic (which can also be signed). In any event, your community provides you with a protective talisman (used in many cultures and times) to take with you.

22.5 You Are Not Alone

Of course, there are recluses and hermits who have separated themselves from society for whatever reason. There are also outcasts and people who have been exiled and ostracized. When babies (animal or human) are separated from their mothers they can wither and die from lack of contact. Being part of a group is almost essential to life. The myriad interest groups that exist are testimony to this. As a therapist it may be important to help your client find a group or groups they can be part of (rather than apart from). (A friend of mine, a sociologist, founded Interaction, a group that helps singles meet in a safe environment. After being a bachelor for many years, he found his life's partner in this group!) Reach out, explore, dare to change. Life is with people.

Chapter Twenty-Three

First- and Second-Order Change and Reframing

23.1 First- and Second-Order Change

From my perspective, one of the most important books ever written was *Change: Principles of Problem Formation and Problem Resolution* (Watzlawick, et al., 1974). The blurb states in part:

> This book deals with the age-old questions of persistence and change in human affairs. More particularly, it is concerned with how problems arise and are perpetuated in some instances, and resolved in others. It examines how, paradoxically, common sense and logical approaches often fail and in doing so compound an existing problem, while seemingly "illogical" and "unreasonable" actions succeed in producing the desired change. [...] It incorporates concepts of human communication, interactional (i.e. marital and family) therapy, the pathogenic and therapeutic effects of paradoxes (double binds), and of action-oriented rather than origin-oriented techniques of problem resolution. While the book draws some of its examples from the field of psychotherapy, its premises regarding problem formation and resolution are applicable in the much wider and more general areas of human interaction, including large social systems and even international relations

Wow! How is all of this possible in a book published four decades ago?

The first three chapters of the book set the logical framework for the rest of the book. They discuss three ways in which problems are created and maintained by mishandling: (1) action is necessary, but is not taken; (2) action is taken when it should not be; and (3) action is taken at the wrong (logical) level.

There are two orders of change. *First-order change* occurs *within* the system and is characterized by doing more of the same. This is typically the way problems are handled by parents and institutions. When a child misbehaves a punishment is meted out. When the child misbehaves more, then the punishment is increased. This, of course, ignores the observation that the initial punishment has not worked since the child misbehaves again! Escalation of punishment does not work, except for some children when it is so draconian that it terrifies them into behaving. When does the punishment of the child become out of proportion to the misbehavior, and is this the way you wish to raise your children? (If it does not work, then do something else.)

Institutions like the government and the military favor first-order change. If a certain amount of money and resources have been poured into a particular project without success, then the government tends to spend more money in that area. The most egregious example of this is the succession of "wars" on drugs. Prison terms and fines and interdictions keep escalating, without any noticeable reduction in drug usage or the crime associated with it. More of the same has not worked in this area, and about one half of the enormous prison population in the U.S. is there on drug-related crimes. Something different needs to be done.

Before discussing second-order change it should be pointed out that countries like Japan and Singapore do not have the drink-driving problem of the U.S. because their laws are so severe in this regard. Drink-driving simply should not be tolerated!

Second-order change is *meta* to or external to the system. Watzlawick, et al. (pp. 82–83), make four comments about second-order change:

1. Second-order change is applied to what in the first-order change perspective appears to be a solution, because in the second-order change perspective this "solution" reveals itself as the keystone of the problem whose solution is attempted.

2. While first-order change always appears to be based on common sense (the "more of the same" recipe), second-order change appears weird, unexpected, and uncommon-sensical; there is a puzzling, paradoxical element in the process of change.

3. Applying second-order change techniques to the "solution" means that the situation is dealt with in the here and now. These techniques deal with effects and not with their presumed causes; the crucial question is *what?* and not *why?*

4. The use of second-order change techniques lifts the situation out of the paradox-engendering trap created by the self-reflexiveness of the attempted solution and places it in a different frame.

A major contribution from thinking about first- and second-order change is its ability to illuminate societal problems as well as personal ones. In the next two sections we briefly discuss paradoxes and reframing, both second-order change tactics, as ways of working interpersonally.

23.2 Paradoxes

Chapter 6 in *Change* (pp. 62–71) is on the use of paradoxes. One of the classic examples of this is the request to "be spontaneous." An example is, "I want you to want to clean up your room." This imposes the rule that behavior should not be rule-compliant, but spontaneous. The insomniac who *tries* to fall asleep by exerting willpower cannot succeed since falling asleep is a natural phenomenon which can only occur spontaneously. So, paradoxically the insomniac can be given the instruction to "try to stay awake" or to "stay awake as long as possible." Remember that the word "try" implies failure. "Try to behave better." "Now, really *try* to have an orgasm the next time you have sex." Another class of paradoxical interventions is to *prescribe the symptom*. "You really ought to **wash your hands more often**." (You can fill in endless compulsive tasks and behaviors in place of the bold-faced phrase.) Also note that *paradoxical intention* was one of the interventions developed by Viktor Frankl in his system of Logotherapy.

23.3 Reframing

In the introduction to Chapter 8 (op cit., pp. 92–109) on the gentle art of reframing, the example is used about how Tom Sawyer got his friends to *want* to whitewash the fence that was one of his chores. Whitewashing was reframed into being something wonderful and desirable! To quote about reframing (p. 95):

> To reframe, then, means to change the conceptual and/or emotional setting or viewpoint in relation to which a situation is experienced and to place it in another frame which fits the "facts" of the same concrete situation equally well or even better, and thereby changes its entire meaning. [...] any opinion (or view, attribution of meaning, and the like) is *meta* to the object of this opinion or view, and therefore is of the next higher logical level.

They also quote the philosopher St Epictetus of the first century AD: "It is not the things themselves which trouble us, but the opinions that we have about these things." So it is how we *perceive* the "facts," and these perceptions are subject to change via reframing. In a sense, being stuck means that you are not able to think of other ways of reacting or thinking. When you cannot figure out a puzzle or a riddle it can be quite frustrating. Yet, once you know the solution you are not fooled by that puzzle again. You know the answer and with reframing you know other ways of responding. Another aspect of reframing is that it operates on the level of meta-reality, where change takes place even if the objective circumstances of a situation are beyond human control.

In my observations at conferences of "master" therapists doing demonstrations I found that it was possible to characterize in almost all of the demonstrations that what they were doing was some form of reframing, i.e. changing the perspective of the volunteer. The ability to reframe seemed to be second nature to them, no matter what approach they were demonstrating! The last stanza in Robert Burns's "To a Louse" speaks to reframing:

> O wad some Power the giftie gie us
> To see oursels as ithers see us!
> It wad frae mony a blunder free us,
> An' foolish notion:

What airs in dress an' gait wad lea'e us,
An' ev'n devotion!

This is an interesting reframe which I use from time to time by asking a client to step outside of herself and view herself from another perspective or from the viewpoint of another person. That is, "to see ourselves as others see us." This "wad frae mony a blunder free us"! The Gestalt Therapy two-chair process does this in another way.

Reframing, from my perspective and observation and experience, is the most effective change agent I have come across.

23.4 Exemplifications

Under this title, Chapter 10 (op cit., pp. 116–157) illustrates second-order change approaches under the following headings:

1. Less of the Same
2. Making Overt the Covert
3. Advertising Instead of Concealing
4. The Great Effects of Small Causes
5. The "Bellac Ploy"
6. Utilizing Resistance
7. Unchallengeable Accusations and Unprovable Denials
8. Benevolent Sabotage
9. The Benefits of Inattention
10. Study Problems
11. Dealing with Utopias
12. The "Devil's Pact"

All of these approaches are well worth studying and adding to your set of skills. The case examples are fascinating, to say the least. In this section I will present only one of them in some detail and that is the one on utilizing resistance.

Utilizing Resistance –The basic approach is to reframe resistance as a precondition for, or even as an aspect of, change. This appears to be nonsensical. An essential question asked of the client is, "Why should you change?" They will have to puzzle over this. The next question might be, "How could you possibly change?" This is a challenge, and the paradoxical intervention of choice is "Go slow!"

This directive implies that they will be changing, and that they can safely do this s-l-o-w-l-y. In fact, the "go slow!" intervention can usefully be combined with the prescription for a relapse. (Please note that prescribing and predicting a relapse is generally a safe thing to do in that it is a bind. If they relapse, you have predicted it, and it is therefore an okay thing to do. If they do not, then they have successfully begun the change process.)

With clients who are "visitors" (they are there because their presence has been mandated in some way by parents, spouses, or legal authorities), the resistance to change is palpable and can also be overt. Such a client may be told that there is nothing that can be done about his situation, except possibly to teach him how to live with it. Being a "born loser" in whatever system he is stuck in means that he is doomed to forever messing things up in his life. You, as the therapist, might be a bit sad about that, but such is life. The person is challenged, given a prognosis, and forced to think about choices.

With resistant clients there are two things to keep in mind. The first is that resistance is in the mind of the therapist. One of the NLP presuppositions is that there is no such thing as a resistant client, there are only therapists who are limited in what they feel they can do. The second is to keep in mind that in judo you use a person's strength and resistance to win. The parallel in psychotherapy is to utilize the resistance to help the person change. After all, therapists like Milton Erickson loved clients who were "resistant."

23.5 Change

In concluding this chapter I cite Mary Goulding's typical opening remark to an individual client or to a group:

What are you willing to change today?

Think about this apparently simple question. There is a presupposition and expectation on the therapist's part that the client will find something to change today. After all, they have come to see you, a therapist, and the implication is that they are stuck in some way and are there to get help from you in getting past this place. The question starts an internal search for what they are *willing* to change today. The client now has the choice of deciding whether that will be something trivial or something more significant. And once they have responded with a particular concern, they have effectively committed themselves to a change in that concern. Please also note that this question belongs in the class of statements called "binds," in which the respondent is bound to do something different. In face-to-face therapy it is amazing what one sentence can do!

Chapter Twenty-Four

Ideomotor Signaling

24.1 Chevreul's Pendulum and Finger Signaling

The French chemist Michel Eugène Chevreul was the first to report on systematic studies involving the ideomotor use of pendulums (Chevreul, 1833). He was born on 31 August 1786 and died on 9 April 1889, living to 102. He had a distinguished career as a chemist and his 100th birthday was a national event in France. Chevreul correctly interpreted the ideomotor movements which set the pendulum in motion as being due to micromuscular movements caused by the unconscious thoughts of the subject. It is this direct access to the unconscious mind that makes the use of the Chevreul pendulum (and other ideomotor signals) so powerful and useful.

The pendulum is made from any light object (nut, bolt, lead fishing sinker, plastic sphere) tied to something easy to grasp like a button, using a thread (nylon dental floss is excellent for this). The thread is 8–10 inches long and is held between two fingers with the arm supported on a table or chair arm. The weight moves in perpendicular directions in response to the person thinking or responding to yes/no questions. A third response of the pendulum moving in a circle was initially "maybe," but this was chosen too frequently. The third response is currently used as "not willing (or ready) to answer now," a better formulation.

Responses are faster when ideomotor finger signals are used. One finger denotes "yes," one "no," and the third is for "not willing to answer now." For ease of working with clients I typically pick the index finger to be "yes," the middle finger to be "no," and the thumb for the third response. If the finger or pendulum movement is volitional (client wishing to please or...), the movements are smooth and fairly large. Micromuscular unconscious movements are hesitant and jerky and can be quite small. The yes/no/not ready responses are obtained from doing something like playing "20 Questions" with the client. This will be discussed in the next section when presenting David Cheek's contributions.

For completeness we will mention here that there are other forms of ideomotor or ideodynamic movements and responses. A common one is the automatic raising of your hand to shake hands when meeting someone. Head nods in conversation are quite noticeable and can be slight or vigorous. Everyone who has lectured to a group knows that there are always some audience members who are nodders. This is sometimes reassuring and sometimes annoying. Automatic writing and drawing are ideomotor responses. The Ouija board, which is occasionally used, is also controlled by ideomotor movements, but of several people in coordination. Body shifts and movements are ideodynamic as they are apparently occurring outside of conscious volition.

24.2 David B. Cheek's Contributions

David B. Cheek was an obstetrician/gynecologist who used hypnosis in his work quite early. His book with LeCron (Cheek and LeCron, 1968) is a classic in the field. The two of them refined the use of ideomotor signaling into an effective therapeutic modality. Cheek wrote the definitive book in this area (Cheek, 1994). Earlier he teamed up with E. L. Rossi in a book that emphasized the use of ideomotor methods in mind–body therapy (Rossi and Cheek, 1988). A description of his approach can be found in Battino and South (Chapter 10, pp. 281–305, 2005).

> In the introduction to Rossi and Cheek, Rossi indicates that there are at least three levels at which mind–body information is encoded. They are: physiological, ideodynamic, and verbal. The ideodynamic level is at the psychobiological level where there are mind–body interactions and memories. Cheek's clinical hypothesis is that ideomotor signaling reaches deeper into the psychobiological matrix to access sources of mind–body healing which are not

usually or easily available to verbally oriented psychotherapy. Cheek's publications and the material and demonstrations presented in his workshops (several of which I attended) give credence to his hypothesis. His approach to mind–body healing has no side-effects, of course.

The methods that Cheek developed are relatively simple and involve careful questioning. After explaining about finger signaling, Cheek proceeds in the following *retrospective* approach (adapted from Rossi and Cheek, 1988, p. 29):

Steps for Ideomotor Signaling Approach

1. *Accessing a Problem*
   a. Is there some past event responsible for your concern? (If the answer is no, ask if there could be a group of events.)
   b. Was it before you were twenty years old? Ten years old? Ask until you get a year.
   c. Please review what is happening at that time. When you know what it is, your yes finger will lift, the memory will come back, and you will be able to talk about it.
2. *Therapeutic Reframing*
   a. Is it okay to tell me about it? (If yes, have the client tell you about the memories.)
   b. Is there an earlier experience that may have set the stage or made you vulnerable to what you just told me? (If yes, go back to Step 1.)
3. *Ratifying Therapeutic Gains*
   a. Now that you know this, can you be well (or resolve this problem)? (A no response means that additional insight and reframing is needed as in Steps 1 and 2 above.)
   b. Is there anything else we need to know so that you can be free of this problem? (If the problem cannot be completely resolved at this time, then go to the next step.)
   c. You can now let your inner mind give you a "yes" signal when it is ready to give you a

date in your mind now of a completely satis-
factory resolution of this problem.

Please note several things about this procedure:

- Whenever you get a finger movement, acknowledge it by saying appropriately, "Yes/no/not
  ready. Thank you." This ratifies that you noticed
  the finger movement.
- Be aware that ideomotor movements are typically
  small and hesitant or jerky.
- When this procedure is used the client typically
  goes into some level of trance. (This happens
  whenever a person "goes inside.") The depth is
  not important.
- The process is not silent, in the sense that the therapist does all of the talking. You can request and
  receive verbal information from the client at various stages of the process.
- The critical comment is in Step 3a, which needs to
  be elaborated on. Since the client is going back in
  her mind to the initiating event(s) which occurred
  in the past and now she is in the future (present
  time) where she has more perspective, resources,
  experience and knowledge, the implication is that
  she is well beyond that earlier event and no longer needs to be troubled by it. (This is a kind of
  reframe.)
- The entire process takes 15–20 minutes.

What has been described above is primarily for mental health
concerns. That is, it involves "healing" in the sense that I use it.
Some physical concerns can surprisingly yield to this process. I
use ideomotor finger signaling for myself and teach it to clients to
ask questions related to physical symptoms in their bodies. When
they are in a relaxed or meditative state they can ask their body if
this particular pain or symptom is something to worry about in
the sense that they need to see a medical doctor or take a particular medicine or seek physical therapy, for example. (This is related
to the bioenergetic analysis dictum of "the body never lies.") My

volunteer work is with people who have life-challenging diseases. People who have an active cancer or are in remission get very concerned (and rightly so) when a new pain appears or one recurs. It is comforting to know that they can query their body in this regard.

In addition to the above, Cheek made some other contributions which are noted here. As a surgeon he was quite aware that patients could hear what was said in an operating room. He was therefore quite careful about what was said in the OR. Healing messages were given to the patient during operations. Cheek believed that people could hear and understand what was said (at some level) *in utero* and during birth, and that they could recall this via ideomotor finger signaling. Whether this actually occurs or is projection, Cheek accessed these natal and birth memories via finger signals and suggested to the person that in looking back from the present they could understand and forgive what may have been unintentional or inadvertent negative messages. He cited many cases where accessing and working with these earliest "memories" were helpful to clients. I should state here that I have done this on rare occasions with clients to good effect.

Ideomotor signaling is a fast and effective way to help clients out of stuck places, although it is not frequently used today. The next section is about two of Cheek's students who actively use ideomotor signals in their current practices.

24.3 *Ewin and Eimer's Work with Ideomotor Signals*

Dabney Ewin, M.D. and Bruce Eimer, Ph.D. were both students and colleagues of David Cheek. Their book (Ewin and Eimer, 2006) is indeed a "how-to" manual for using ideomotor methods. From a quick scan of their list of references there does not appear to be many recent books or papers on ideomotor approaches. This is unfortunate because from my experience and perspective they are some of the most effective and efficient ways of doing therapy. In the preface they state that the book is about using ideomotor (IM) signals for the rapid hypnoanalysis of psychosomatic disorders. The book emphasizes the use of IM with clients who have psychosomatic concerns. The word "hypnoanalysis" indicates that they also emphasize the use of hypnosis and psychodynamic approaches. As mentioned earlier in this chapter, any time that IM is used with a client the client typically enters a hypnotic state. Ewin and Eimer's style of working with clients means that they are concerned with the origins of present-day concerns (as was Cheek) and that their way of using IM is influenced by this.

Perhaps the most controversial aspect of the authors' work (and that of Cheek himself) is their belief that valid memories could be obtained for events not only before the age of three, but also even birth and intrauterine memories. The many case histories in this book and the transcripts of sessions give some credence to this belief. Regardless, it is a useful expectation.

The authors clearly state in the introduction (p. xix), "Our technique helps us uncover and reframe the pathogenic fixed idea/s underlying the patient's problem and symptoms. We have found by analyzing when and where the symptom started, and under what circumstances, we have been able to achieve long-term cures for many presenting problems in five visits. [...] We view it as our job to find the reason and reframe it—to appropriately *re-interpret* the need for the presenting dysfunctional behavior."

The book is divided into three parts: Basic Concepts; Basic Applications; and Annotated Clinical Session Transcripts. The first five chapters deal with the basics, such as ideomotor signals, principles of hypnotherapy, and how to set up ideomotor signals. An item of practical value has to do with their practice of designating three fingers for the responses of "Yes," "No," and "I don't know," or "I don't want to answer yet." This makes it easier to remember client responses. They will also stroke a finger to reinforce responses, and always acknowledge a response. Their last signal is, "If anything crosses your mind that you want to talk about, or if you want to ask a question, just raise your hand and we'll talk." This enhances participation.

In Part II basic applications are discussed and illustrated. The exploration into past causes leads to making statements to the client like, "Would it be all right with your subconscious mind to just turn it off, and leave it in the past?" This is generally followed with, "Then do it. Want it to happen, let it happen, and it will happen." This simple directive to leave things in the past that have outlived their usefulness and are no longer relevant is a cornerstone of this kind of work. In my experience and theirs, clients do just that!

The annotated clinical sessions are worthwhile studying if only for the authors' elegant and careful use of language. They have obviously honed their technique to an effective and efficient approach. (The annotated cases are too long to reproduce any parts here.) The appendixes are full of practical information such as: a detailed intake and worksheet, how to set up ideomotor signals, and an ideomotor analysis worksheet.

24.4 A Confession

I have long been an admirer of David Cheek and his work. I hope that shows in this chapter.

Chapter Twenty-Five

Psychodrama

25.1 Introduction

Psychodrama is still alive and performing. Before writing something about it and how it continues to be relevant to doing good therapy, let me just cite a few recent books which you can consult (Moreno, 1972; Holmes, et al., 1994; Karp, et al., 1998; Dayton and Moreno, 2005).

Jacob L. Moreno, M.D., developed psychodrama in Vienna in 1914 through working with children; telling them stories, and listening to their stories. He decided to throw away the script because, "The idea is the encounter between people, and the area between people." He brought psychodrama to the United States, where he met his future wife, Zerka, in 1941. They developed this approach until his death in 1974 and she has continued this work. Zerka has said, "We are all natural role players on the stage of life; some do better than others. And the ones we don't do so well in, they need a little help. And you do them best, not by repetition but by doing them spontaneously and with creativity."

Psychodrama is always done with an audience. A person volunteers to be the protagonist, tells something about her life, and then the director sets the scene with the help of the protagonist. An episode from her life is acted out. If it is not done to the protagonist's satisfaction, then it can be redone with her modifications. The protagonist may be one of the actors. To aid in the movement of the drama one of the leaders (or an experienced person) can "double" by standing behind or beside an actor and offering lines (suggestions). Rather than talking about one's life and concerns, immediacy is given to the client's situation by acting out what she thinks is going on in her life. In addition to the characters in the drama, inanimate objects can be given roles. This could be a wall or a rock or a building or a piece of furniture. The drama continues until a resolution develops. It is the "magic" of psychodrama that a resolution tends to appear quite quickly.

There are five instruments in a psychodrama: (1) the director; (2) the primary ego or protagonist; (3) the auxiliary ego; (4) a group presence; and (5) the setting. The director warms up the group, and the personality of the therapist is the tool, with every therapist being different. Moreno did not believe that language is the royal route to the psyche. He said, "Things happen between human beings on the primordial level, lying below language, and that's what I want to tap." The director establishes a safe place for the protagonist and group members. The protagonist shows how the auxiliary should act by taking on that role first.

The *auxiliary ego* is the person who represents the absentee who cannot come, doesn't want to come, is not available, and may not even be therapeutic at this point. (Trained actors are used to represent the auxiliary ego nowadays, but other patients and group members were used in the beginning.) It is acted at first as it is perceived by the protagonist, and then as it might be beyond perception. The auxiliary ego can be anything: a body part, a delusion, a relation, an animal. Role reversal is important, not as a therapeutic tool for the protagonist, but as a diagnostic tool for the director. In *doubling* you are beside the antagonist and coach him/her with statements to say.

In psychodrama it is felt that life is not replicated. They go beyond life as it is. There are exchanges you cannot have with your mother or other people. The relationship between the protagonist and the auxiliary ego is beyond empathy and beyond transference. It's built on the reality that may be buried somewhere and then brought to light in the action. Real people are not being dealt with. Rather, it is the perceptions people have of *other* people, and perception is subject to change. Psychodrama is not lineal; it is totally non-lineal, which means you can go wherever out there; therefore, within a psychodrama the director has to be the most spontaneous person in the group.

There are training institutes in the U.S. and overseas in psychodrama. You really need to experience psychodrama and get training in it to be able to use it proficiently.

A final thought: The Morenos felt that the unlived life was not worth examining, so it needs to be lived as fully as you can.

25.2 Dream Work

I do not know how much dream work is done at the present time, or even if it fits into approaches like CBT. In my private practice dreams rarely show up since I do not ask for them. A number of years ago I met an American Jungian therapist from Switzerland and we got talking. I discovered that he had many clients and that he typically saw them for several years; in fact, he told me that he occasionally had clients where they would spend several years discussing one dream! I did not let on how astounding this was to me. We did have an interesting conversation, though!

At that time my experience with dream work came out of my training in Gestalt Therapy. Dreams were one of the things we worked on in our group settings. The person in the hot seat would tell his dream. The leader would then set the stage with characters and objects from the dream. Sometimes the person would be on stage, and sometimes off stage, observing and commenting and directing. The dream, with its animate and inanimate parts, was brought to life. In observing and participating in his dream the protagonist would have the opportunity to say and do things that were relevant to his life situation. Out of this drama came perspectives, insights and resolutions that were quite effective because they came out of his "real" life situation as performed in the drama. You have to participate in such an experience to appreciate how powerful it can be as a change agent.

Early in my training I was fortunate to take a ten-week workshop with Meredith Dallas ("Dal") in Yellow Springs. Dal was on the Antioch College theater faculty, a director and actor, and had trained in Gestalt Therapy. We all got to work on our dreams, and it was a fascinating and productive experience.

25.3 Commentary

Although it may be difficult to find a training group in psychodrama or a workshop where you can experience it first-hand, it is worth trying. You really need training and experience to use psychodrama in your practice. What you can take away from reading about psychodrama is the knowledge that group work can be enhanced by adding elements of drama, like acting out a scene from a client's life.

Chapter Twenty-Six

Solution-Focused Brief Therapy

26.1 Introduction

Solution-focused therapy probably started with Milton Erickson, as have so many innovative approaches. The man who developed it systematically with research and in his many books was Steve de Shazer. His wife, Insoo Kim Berg, was also instrumental in its promulgation and development. They worked at the Brief Family Therapy Center of Milwaukee (BFTC). I recall a workshop I attended with de Shazer in which he contrasted problem-oriented therapy with solution-oriented (or focused) therapy. His opening comment was something like, "Would you prefer spending your days as a therapist with client after client talking about their problems and miseries, or would you rather spend time with clients talking about what went well or worked in their lives?" The *problem* with problem-oriented therapies is that clients can talk endlessly about their problems since they think that that is what you want to hear and that is what you are being paid for. They will also tell you endlessly about why they behave the way they do, and why they are stuck in their present impasses. The Freudian emphasis on digging into the past to find out the whys of present behaviors and emotions is based on the false assumption that knowing why will free you from what troubles you. If this were the case, then listening to a client's recital of the whys is all that you would need to do! In effect, clients would be self-healing via the "why" route. Yet, this seldom works in practice and in life. We were sold a bill of goods over one century ago that persists and persists.

As a current example, I spent some time recently with a relative on the phone attempting to convince him that knowing "why" a woman he was interested in was behaving the way she did was a fruitless endeavor. His being curious would not change the situation or her. Although it is a human trait to want to understand the *why* of the world and people around us, this works well in the realm of science, but not so well in interpersonal relations. You can be sad about how a particular person responds to you. In the end I believe that you just have to accept such behavior without knowing why and just walk away from the situation. In another recent example, a friend wanted to know why I had done a particular thing in respect to him. I had my reasons I guess. To me it was a straightforward interaction, and he would not accept that since he was looking for deeper and perhaps more sinister reasons. Rather than accept this on the surface level (where most of these things are best accepted), it took a long time to be able to connect again as friends.

When you ask for "exceptions" to a client's stuck behavior you are eliciting from their lives what they have already done that is a "solution" to their presenting problem. That is, there have been occasions in the past week or two when they were not depressed/panicked/anxious/lonely/compelled to do a particular activity/sad. A study by Weiner-Davis, de Shazer, and Gingerich (1987) showed that when clients were asked about beneficial or useful changes that had occurred between the time they made the appointment and the appointment itself, most clients reported useful changes. Ask and ye shall be given solution-focused information. Then you can build on these beginnings from the person's life. They may feel that they have been doomed to being forever miserable, yet here they are telling you about some good stuff.

I so like the three guiding principles of solution-focused therapy that I am going to repeat them here:

- If it isn't broken, don't fix it.
- If it has worked once, do it again.
- If it doesn't work, then don't do it again—do something different.

One of the things I like about this approach is that it is so common-sensical.

Before continuing in this chapter, here are a few references: de Shazer (1985, 1988, 1991, 1994); Miller and Berg (1995); Miller,

Hubble, and Duncan (1996); Hubble, Duncan, and Miller (1999), and Berg and Dolan (2001).

26.2 As-If and the Miracle Question

As-If applies to behavior and the Miracle Question applies to thinking. There have been studies done on actors acting *as-if* they were sad, happy, angry, depressed, etc. Various physiological measurements were made during their acting, like oxygen usage, heart rate, skin resistance, saliva content, blood pressure, etc. These measurements were also carried out on people who were diagnosed with the same mental states. The actors exhibited the same physiological responses as those with the "real" mental state! So, acting as-if you were anxious creates a concomitant physical and mental state.

A recent client of mine told me that she *decided* to be "happy" and that her life had improved significantly based on that decision. She was now acting as-if her life was a happy one. How can you use this in a therapeutic situation?

One of the interventions developed by the authors of *Change* (Watzlawick, et al., 1990) for working with couples illustrates the as-if intervention. The couple was asked if they were willing to do an experiment; they said yes. The experiment was that one of them (say, the wife) would flip a coin each evening. If the coin came up heads, then on the next day she would act as-if everything was going okay in their marriage. If the coin came up tails, then she would behave "normally" the next day. She was to keep records of this and so was her husband (who did not know which side of the coin came up). When they returned two weeks later they were asked about what had changed in their lives. Typically, their life had improved significantly, and after a few days the husband could not really tell whether the coin had come up heads or tails the previous evening! This coin-toss procedure can also be used with individuals and easily adapted. The person or couple needs to be intrigued into attempting this experiment.

People do get tired of living the same humdrum life and being in a rut. Why not do an experiment?

Insoo Kim Berg learned about the Miracle Question intervention from a client, who had wondered aloud about how her life would change if a miracle occurred. Berg recognized the power of this idea and developed it further. Here's how it works. After doing an intake and actively listening to the client discuss why they are there, then waiting for the client to wind down in this recitation, the Miracle Question can be proposed. The client has been heard, notes have been taken, and the client has indicated what they want out of therapy. The Miracle Question is:

> Suppose that tonight while you are asleep that a miracle occurs. The miracle is that what you came to talk with me about today is solved to your satisfaction. This is a miracle. When you wake up tomorrow morning, what is the first thing you will notice that will let you know the miracle has occurred?

For the next twenty to thirty minutes (or more), lead the client to give you as much detail as you can get about what it is that has already changed in their life post-miracle. Elicit behaviors and actions rather than feelings. That is, it is not so much about how their feelings have changed as what they are *doing* differently, and what it is that others notice about them. How would you be going about getting ready for work differently? If you were to step outside of yourself, what would you notice about the way that you stand and move? What would your spouse/children notice? When you are at work, what would your co-workers notice that lets them know there is something different about you? As you watch yourself in interactions with people who know you (and others), what do you notice about your behavior and posture and ways of reacting? What would they notice? Perhaps in the evening you call a relative who knows you well—what would they notice about the way you interact with them on the phone? The more *detail* you can get about how their life has changed post-miracle, the more real it becomes to them. In a way, this is an elaborate reframing of their life that they are carrying out! They tell you what is different and, as in all reframing, this new perspective changes their perceptions about themselves. The changes you observe can be miraculous!

The Miracle Question and variants of it are some of the most frequent things that I do with clients. It works, and it works rapidly. There is, of course, much more to solution focused brief therapy than I presented here.

Chapter Twenty-Seven

Narrative Therapy

27.1 Introduction

Narrative Therapy has been around for about twenty-four years, after the initial publication describing it by the late Michael White (an Australian) and David Epston (a New Zealander) (White and Epston, 1990). They described a fascinating way to do therapy that involved the community and people's stories. Before giving you a brief discussion in the next section of what they developed here are two additional useful references: (Freedman and Combs,1996; White, 2007). In addition to other books in the field, the websites of the Dulwich Centre where White worked contain much information: <www.dulwichcentre.com.au> <www.narrativetherapy library.com>

It is worthwhile noting that White and Epston arrived at Narrative Therapy from a grounding in social, linguistic, and communication theory. They give the following eight ideas as being part of the narrative method of thinking (p. 83):

1.   Privileges the person's lived experiences.
2.   Encourages a perception of a changing world through the plotting or linking of lived experience through the temporal dimension.
3.   Invokes the subjunctive mood in the triggering of presuppositions, the establishment of implicit meaning, and in the generation of multiple perspective.
4.   Encourages polysemy (polyphonic orientation) and the use of ordinary, poetic and picturesque language in the

description of experience and in the endeavor to construct new stories.

5. Invites a reflexive posture and an appreciation of one's participation in interpretive acts.

6. Encourages a sense of authorship and re-authorship of one's life and relationships in the telling and retelling of one's story.

7. Acknowledges that stories are co-produced and endeavors to establish conditions under which the "subject" becomes the privileged author.

8. Consistently inserts pronouns "I" and "you" in the description of events.

27.2 Narrative Therapy

With the overview above I am just going to write here about two aspects of Narrative Therapy: externalization and letters. A basic tenet of this approach which was not mentioned above is their credo that "The person is not the problem; the problem is the problem." This gets away from the medical model with its limiting diagnoses of the person having this named DSM thing or that one. A person is unique and individual, and at this point in time may be having some difficulties in their life. Let us then deal with their current concerns and not saddle them with a label which designates them as a dysfunctional entity who needs to be "repaired" by some predetermined "evidence-based" protocol. Erickson found that dealing with *symptoms* in terms of removing them was effective, and he did this without labels! If the client were the problem, then symptom removal would not work.

Externalization

This is perhaps the best known method that narrative therapists use, and it is well suited to doing brief therapy. The following quote by the Canadian therapist Karl Tomm, to be found in O'Hanlon (O'Hanlon, 1994) is illuminating:

> Ironically, this technique [externalization] is both very simple and extremely complicated. It is simple in the

sense that what it basically entails is a linguistic separation of the problem from the personal identity of the patient. What is complicated and difficult is the delicate means by which it is achieved. It is through the therapist's careful use of language in the therapeutic conversation that the person's healing initiatives are achieved. [...] What is new about the narrative approach is that it provides a purposeful sequence of questions that consistently produce a freeing effect for people.

Narrative therapists are adept at using careful language and questions. Freedman and Combs (1996, pp. 113–143) give a systematic development of the use of questions with many illustrations.

In one of my books (Battino, 2002, pp. 269–270) I wrote about externalization:

The process of externalization—with a person or a family—begins with coming up with a mutually acceptable *name* for the externalized problem. Are you being controlled or tricked by: Anger, Fear, Depression, Paranoia, Anxiety, Urine, Fatty Food, Bulimia, Panic, Anorexia? How long has this been going on? Have there been times when you were able to resist _____? Put it in its place? Ignore it? Tell it off? This linguistically separates the person from the problem label, and clients soon perceive their problem in this externalized way. To aid in this separation the ogre or demon is made more real by attributing to it evil intentions and tactics. This is a nasty entity who has it in for you, and who has made your life a misery in many ways—elicit those ways from the client.

I continued (p. 271) as follows:

If the person is not the problem, and the problem is the problem, then separating the person from the problem via externalization is an essential step in moving from what the client considers to be involuntary and uncontrollable behavior to voluntary and controllable behavior. Narrative therapists cleverly personify the controlling element to make it real in an AS-IF sense. (Is this an adaptation of racial memories of being possessed by demons, dybbuks, and evil spirits? Certainly it connects with the hero's journey. Is then narrative therapy a kind of modern-day exorcism? These parallels make for useful speculation...) Once the problem has been externalized, then in a solution-focused-brief-therapy sense *exceptions* to being controlled are sought. These exceptions, times when the "demon" has been thwarted or resisted, are the basis for the client's new life story; that is, the new story is built on the client's proven strengths and resources. "What will let you continue to ignore/thwart/overcome/restrict Depression (for example)?" "What can you do to put Depression in its place so it will no longer bother you?"

When I present these ideas to clients they are quite receptive. The "exorcism" or removal of the controlling internal influence is generally carried out in a short hypnosis session which incorporates the client's ideas about how to do this. That is, they tell me what stronger countervailing force will rid them of the enemy within.

Letters

They are used in a variety of ways and quite extensively in Narrative Therapy. In fact, White and Epston devote an entire chapter to this (1990, pp. 77–187). The following is a brief list of the kinds of letters used:

- Letters of invitation—engage or entice people into therapy
- Redundancy letters—show that a client is no longer needed in a certain role
- Letters of prediction—they predict outcomes and behaviors
- Counter-referral letters—emphasize development in a narrative sense
- Letters for special occasions—ratify comment on special occasions and ratify progress
- Brief letters—reassuring letters for people relatively socially isolated
- End of session—therapist's notes at the end of a session

Narrative therapists classically send a copy of their session notes to their clients after the session is over. Thus, both the client and therapist have a record of what went on in the session. These letters may also contain predictions.

One of the special features of narrative therapy that I like is the giving of diplomas or certificates of accomplishment to clients at the end of treatment (and occasionally during treatment). I have special parchment like paper I use for this. A typical certificate may state, "This is to certify that _____ has successfully _____ ." What a wonderful gift to a departing client!

Chapter Twenty-Eight

Hypnosis

28.1 Introduction

I am convinced that Milton H. Erickson, M.D., single-handedly brought hypnosis into the twentieth century from its scattered history in the nineteenth century. Sigmund Freud had traveled to Paris and studied hypnosis there. He found it to be quite useful. After returning to Vienna he effectively gave it up in favor of working with free association, analysis, dreams, and childhood roots of neuroses. It was not until Erickson actively worked to study, write, research, and lecture on hypnosis in the 1920s and in subsequent decades that hypnosis had a rebirth in the U.S., and later overseas. At this time of writing, the Milton H. Erickson Foundation has about 150 affiliated institutes worldwide; in the last few decades most of this growth has been outside the U.S. All of these institutes have been vetted by the Foundation and are considered to be reliable. The periodic Erickson Congresses are attended by up to 1000 professionals, and they involve training and an amazing variety of workshops and demonstrations and conversation hours. Visit the Foundation website at www.erickson-foundation.org for information on their activities, the affiliated institutes, and their publications. A free newsletter is available online or in hard copy. Hypnosis is alive and well in the twenty-first century.

In my own private practice I use hypnosis frequently. Even though I am known for this, I am careful to say (following a typical introductory comment that Erickson used), "If hypnosis is appropriate, I will certainly use it." That is, some clients are not interested in hypnosis and it may not be appropriate with a given client or

within a given session. You may be interested in my book on Ericksonian hypnosis with T.L. South as an introduction (Battino and
South, 2005) to the subject.

28.2 Uses of Hypnosis

Hypnosis has been used for a great many concerns and in a great
variety of circumstances. A partial list follows:

- relaxation
- pain control
- habits, e.g. smoking, overeating and weight control
- obsessive-compulsive behavior
- phobias
- mood disorders, e.g. anxiety, depression, panic
- learning, studying, exams
- sports enhancement
- improving skills
- preparation for surgery
- surgery
- psychotherapy
- impotence
- childbirth
- hypertension
- trauma and PTSD

Some hospitals have a hypnotist on their staff to assist with medical concerns. The literature and research on the uses of hypnosis
is vast. It is not some fly-by-night passing exotic approach. Despite
all of the research and advances there are still many myths extant
about hypnosis. Movies and television and books tend to distort
hypnosis for purposes of entertainment. Stage hypnotists are perhaps the worst in this regard.

In my judgment there are only two reputable training groups
for hypnosis in the U.S. They are the Milton H. Erickson Foundation (cited above) and the American Society of Clinical Hypnosis or
ASCH <www.asch.net>.

My working definition of hypnosis is that it is "focused attention." That is, any time your attention is so focused that the world
around you recedes you are in some level of trance. I make no dis-

tinction between hypnosis, self-hypnosis, relaxation, and meditation. They are all examples of deep concentration, be it in music or reading or a movie or in meditation or in sport or when driving. I am sure that all the readers of this book have had the experience of driving home or to work and not recalling whether you stopped at a particular stop sign or traffic light. Or you have been at a movie or a concert or sports event and "woken up" afterwards wondering where the time went! These are common everyday trances. Being in a trance does not mean that you are not aware on some protective level, say, of the traffic around you.

When you visit a hypnotist for a specific purpose an experienced professional will know many ways in which to induce a trance and then help you achieve your goals once you are in it. The methods used are adapted individually. Hypnosis is practical and effective, yet I continue to be surprised and disappointed that not every hospital has a staff hypnotist. I am also concerned that in my experience in the U.S. that hypnosis is not routinely taught in psychotherapy, psychiatry, clinical psychology, and counseling programs. Professional training is available, and I hope that more therapists (of whatever orientation) will avail themselves of it.

28.3 *Hypnosis for Weight Control*

One of the common reasons I am consulted is for weight control. The people who come to see me are overweight by modest amounts, like twenty to forty pounds. They seem to be the ones most concerned about how heavy they are and their inability to do something about it on their own. Invariably they are knowledgeable about diets and weight control programs and even have libraries full of books about these issues. Many have tried weight control programs, and all have tried some form of dieting. Most have seen advertisements for hypnosis programs for weight control that are run by itinerant hypnotists in local hotels. So, the first thing I ask about is what they have tried to control their weight. Please note that I consistently use the phrase "weight control" and not "weight loss." If you lose something you can find it, and the history of most of my clients is this yo-yoing up and down the weight scale. When I know what they have tried, then I know what has *not* worked for them. The following subsections cover the methods that I use.

"Religious" Conversion and Weight Control

This is usually my starting point in talking about weight control, and needs some explanation. Almost everyone I have talked with who has been successful on their own in permanently changing a lifelong habit like smoking or in making a permanent change in their weight essentially tells me the same thing: "One day I just decided that I was going to stop smoking," or, "I just decided that I was going to have a healthier and lighter weight for the rest of my life." Sometimes this change came about as the result of a conversation with their physician. The physician has to "scare" the person strongly enough to have an effect—this works with some people, but not with others. The parallel with the kind of religious conversion that takes place at revival meetings is strong. It is almost as if some internal switch has been pressed and a completely new mental connection has been formed. "I just decided." When I asked for clarification the responses were similar: "Something changed inside me and I knew from that moment on I would never smoke (or be heavy) again." The inner conviction was complete and unalterable. They all described thinking and feeling differently. There was an instant personality change, and they had become a different person.

I explain this phenomenon to my clients. They do not dispute its existence and this leads me to incorporate such a plausible way of changing into the hypnosis session, a sample of which is given below in the transcript in section D. In effect, I am building up an expectation that a rapid change in their way of living and thinking about themselves can occur.

Presentation of Set-Point Theory of Metabolism

Since I feel it is useful to know something about the physiology involved in weight control I tell the client about the set-point theory of metabolism. The basal metabolism in the body is such that it keeps the body on an even keel (homeostasis). That is, if you occasionally overeat, the body reacts in such a way that your metabolism becomes less efficient and you do not put on weight. If you occasionally eat significantly less, then your metabolism becomes more efficient and you do not lose weight. The metabolism has a "set-point" for a particular weight and digesting and processing food. This set-point can be changed in three ways: by exercising significantly more over a period of time, or by eating significantly more (or less) for a long time, or by doing both.

It is difficult for most people to exercise hard enough and consistently enough to have an impact on the set point. The Olympic champion swimmer Michael Phelps swims so hard and so long in practice that he has to take in 10,000 to 12,000 calories per day. Mere mortals are not up to such strenuous activity. Increasing your regular exercising will help, and it has other benefits besides affecting the metabolic set-point. The most effective exercises according to exercise physiologists (such as Covert Bailey) are those using the big muscles in the legs. Jogging, biking, stepping machines, rowing machines, and fast walking use those muscles. Upper body exercises like swimming (unless you are someone like Phelps) do not have much effect on the set-point. When you do these big-muscles-in-the-legs exercises *start gradually*, and then slowly build up the amount that you do. Also, do not do them so fast that you cannot talk with an exercise companion—if you cannot talk, then slow down.

Calories do count, and taking in significantly fewer calories over a period of time will change the set-point. This generally means taking in 1000 to1500 fewer calories per day. One way to get started on eating less is to recommend to your client that she *over-eat* enough the next week to eliminate two to three pounds. This paradoxical recommendation gets the client's attention. You then explain that we all know how to over-eat and take in fewer calories. You can gorge by eating a head of lettuce and take in practically nothing in calories! You can increase the amount of water you drink to get a sensation of fullness for zero calories. This is common sense. Eating smaller portions and taking the time to chew everything thoroughly so that you can actually taste what you are eating is common sense. (I consciously close my eyes for at least one bite of food at each meal and slowly chew it until it liquefies before swallowing.) You do not need to talk about the caloric content of different foods since everybody seems to know this.

However, increasing exercise alone or decreasing food intake alone is not an efficient way to eliminate poundage. Done separately they are effective only *in extremis*. There is a synergistic effect in increasing exercise consistently and decreasing caloric intake consistently. Doing *both* has the greatest impact on changing the set-point. It is always my recommendation to do both since they can be done in moderation to change the set-point.

Safe Haven and What Works For You

In doing change work with hypnosis and also in doing guided imagery work with people who have life-challenging diseases I always ask about a "safe haven." This is a place they can go to in their mind that is real or imaginary where they feel protected and safe. It can also be a healing and learning place. I ask for enough details about the place so that I can weave an accurate description of the place into the hypnosis session (using their words, if possible). The safe havens that people choose are individual and have ranged from their bed at home to Pyramid Lake in Jasper National Park. Some are general, like being in the woods or by the ocean or in an open meadow. Being in the safe haven in their mind provides comfort and protection, as well as an *expectation* that good things will happen while they are there.

Since I am working with metaphors and imagery I want to use *their* internal sense of what will help them change in the way that they desire. This can be something symbolic like healing hands or healing light or a healing presence. It can be a special real person in their life. For religious people it is the divinity, spirit or entity of their choice. For some it can just be my voice and faith that will be with them. The choice is theirs and this makes it especially effective.

Kinesthetic anchors can be used to remind the client of his/her decision to change, and the presence of their chosen support and facilitating entity when they are in a situation or circumstance where they used to respond in the old way. I generally suggest socially acceptable and innocuous things like touching an ear, holding some fingers together, or lightly scratching their head or their chin. This anchor is then rehearsed with the client thinking about an upcoming time when they need to be vigilant, let's say with over-eating. Although kinesthetic anchors seem to be more effective than other anchors, there are other kinds, like hearing a voice with a particular message. The client, on whose session the transcript in this section is based, chose to hear quacking noises in her head when she was tempted to indulge in fattening foods. She wanted to remind herself that she had gotten so overweight that she felt like a waddling duck. The quacking in her head would stop her. Of course, we rehearsed using this anchor and she was delighted by it!

Background for the Weight Control Transcript

The transcript is based mostly on a female client in her sixties whose husband of many years had died several years earlier. I will call her Laura. She picked up excess weight after his death. Her helper was the Lord, and her safe haven was a camping place in the woods near a stream, enhanced by the aroma of bacon cooking. This was related to a happy childhood memory of camping in many places with her family. The quacking ducks are the signal to eat in a healthy manner. Since this hypnosis session was not recorded, the following transcript builds on my experience of creating a hypnosis session based on what the client has told me. Please pay attention to language usage and where pauses have been incorporated (marked by an ellipsis...).

Hypnosis Weight Control Transcript

Well, Laura, I generally like to start out with asking people to pay attention to their breathing. Please find some way of being comfortable, knowing that you can move and adjust your position. Just notice each breath as it comes in and goes out. With each inhale, chest and belly softly rising. And with each exhale, all of those muscles...relaxing. That's right, just one breath at a time. One heartbeat at a time. Slowly, easily, and naturally...This breath and the next one, this heartbeat, and the next one...Occasionally a stray thought may wander through your mind. Notice it, thank it for being there, and then go back to...this breath, and the next one. Slowly, simply, calmly...At this time you have nothing else to concern you; this is your healing and learning time...Continuing to breathe slowly and easily, all of those muscles just relaxing. And your tongue lies loose and free in your mouth; this breath and...Yes. And within your mind now you can just drift off to that camping place. It is the morning, and you can smell the bacon cooking. And there is the sound of water flowing in the stream. There may be a gentle breeze, and the smell of the forest around you. A bird sings somewhere. This breath, and the next one. There is light dappling down through the leaves. The forest floor is sprinkled with light. There is lightness around you, and peace...While you are enjoying being there you may be wondering how this is going to help in changing your lifestyle so that you will be lighter and healthier and more able to do things physically with comfort and ease. In this place and this time you feel the Lord's presence. It is simpler and easier with His help, with His love, with His support...And you can almost sense, can you not, that with His help, His Presence, that somehow, somehow, somewhere inside you a switch has been flipped...a decision has been made. From this time on you will find a lightness of being...The unneeded and extra weight that has been weighing you down and has been in the way, simply and easily and naturally slips and slides away...permanently....At this time you know, you just know deep inside yourself, you will eat just what your body needs, and do so for the rest of your life. That switch has clicked. Old pathways have been eliminated, and new pathways established. In some fashion, some way, your brain has been rewired, your physiology has altered and changed and accommodated to the new you who is emerging...Breathing softly and easily. Enjoying the smells and the sounds and the sense of the forest around you. And the Lord....You know about really tasting your food and eating slowly, taking smaller portions and increasing in a sensible way your exercise regimen. You know that it is okay to think about various foods and see them and even smell them, knowing that that is enough. You know your no. You no longer have to act on those sensations. For not only is the Lord with you, but you also have your quackers, your ducks to quack away at you in the rare times you will be tempted. That is right, is it not?...And there is that other reminder of touching your ear....You do have so much going for you now. Yes and yes....The sound of water tumbling down a stream, the wind lazily moving through treetops, that big white cloud floating lightly up there, an insect buzzing somewhere, a mushroom on the forest floor, rain and wind and lazily falling snowflakes...A baby's bubbling smile and laughter, a cold drink on a hot day, and hot cocoa on a cold day, and...Touching and being touched, loving and being loved, laughing with, that smile, birdsong in the morning...Sunsets and sunrises, the moon in the morning, this moment, this breath, this heartbeat...That inner sense that the switch has been made, that inner conviction that from now on...This breath and the next one...And you should know, Laura, that your mind is somewhat like a tape recorder so that whatever has happened in this session, today, that is useful and helpful to you, for you, will be with you as you need it and when you need it....From time to time you may re-experience and recall it by just finding a quiet place, paying attention to your breathing, and it will be there with you. I want to thank you, Laura, for your trust, your confidence, and your attention....And, when you are ready, you can just take a deep breath or two, blink your eyes, stretch a bit, and come back to this room here and now...Yes and yes and yes....Thank you.

Commentary

This transcript can be adapted to fit your own clients. The induction is relatively short since the comments about paying attention to breathing are interspersed throughout the session. You will find your own places to insert pauses of various lengths. You will also find particular words and phrases to emphasize by marking them out. The hypnosis session with Laura lasted about fifteen minutes. For the "poetic" interlude towards the end of the transcript please use your own imagination, being aware of your client's interests and experiences. I find that it is useful to do this as a transition between the "therapeutic" part of the session and its end. This "distraction" is both calming and gives the listener time to do inner consolidating work. Since I work as a very brief therapist, and my clients know this, one session is generally all that is needed to bring about a permanent change in the client's way of feeling and thinking about herself, and to move into permanent weight control. The idea about the switch and the accompanying "religious conversion" makes sense to people, as most have seen this in others, and may have also experienced it themselves in some context.

Chapter Twenty-Nine

Provocative Therapy

29.1 Introduction and Description

The book on provocative therapy was published thirty-eight years ago. I was fascinated by the book when I read it then and I was even more fascinated when I got hold of some tapes by Frank Farrelly, the lead author. The book is simply titled *Provocative Therapy* (Farrelly and Brandsma, 1974), and there are many wonderfully illuminating case studies with frequent transcripts. Farrelly got into this kind of therapy from working with patients in institutional settings, but provocative therapy is also practical with "ordinary" clients.

The best way to give you a sense of how Farrelly "provokes" clients into health is to quote from his aforementioned book, with occasional comments from me [in these brackets]. We'll start with two central hypotheses (p. 52)

1. If provoked by the therapist (humorously, perceptively, and within the client's own internal frame of reference), the client will tend to move in the opposite direction from the therapist's definition of the client as a person.
2. If urged provocatively by the therapist (humorously and perceptively) to continue his self-defeating, deviant behaviors, the client will tend to engage in self- and other enhancing behaviors more closely approximating the societal norm.

Under a variety of headings (in italics) here are some useful quotes:

People change and grow in response to challenge
We try to provoke a certain specific type of self-anger. (p. 36)

Clients can change if they choose
We assume that clients have not changed because they *will* not, and that clients can change if they choose. (p. 37)

Few people other than therapists really believe that man is not responsible for what he does, that he does not choose but is driven. (p. 39)

No human group ever existed where a right was given without a corresponding obligation. (p. 39)

The client stresses the "I cannot." The provocative therapist firmly believing that the client *will* not, humorously agrees and echoes the doom and gloom messages of psychological determinism in an attempt to provoke the client into admitting that he is not functioning because he will not. (p. 41)

Clients have far more potential for achieving adaptive, productive, and socialized modes of living than they or most clinicians assume. (p. 41)

The psychological fragility of patients is vastly overrated both by themselves and others. (p. 42) [This is a central tenet of provocative therapy and this observation is important.]

The client's maladaptive, unproductive, antisocial attitudes and behaviors can be drastically altered whatever the degree of severity or chronicity. (p. 43)

Adult or current experiences are as at least if not more significant than childhood or previous experiences in shaping client values, operational attitudes, and behaviors. (p. 44)

The client's behavior with the therapist is a relatively accurate reflection of his habitual patterns of social and interpersonal relationships. (p. 46)

People make sense; the human animal is exquisitely logical and understandable. (p. 47)

The expression of therapeutic hate and joyful sadism toward clients can markedly benefit the client. (p. 48) [Farrelly's faith and experience.]

The following long quote is an essential statement and description about how provocative therapy works (p. 58):

In provocative therapy the therapist points out in a variety of ways either implicitly or explicitly the social consequences of the client's attitudes and behaviors. The therapist attempts to verbalize all the taboo things that people cannot say in our culture to one another; he endeavors to *express the unutterable, feel the unfeelable,* and *think the unthinkable* with the client, verbalizing all the client's implicit doubts, echoing the client's worst thoughts and fears about himself and about the reactions of other people toward him. The client invariably finds that he is not "destroyed or annihilated" and can deal with these conflict areas on a more conscious, realistic, and adaptive basis. [Wow. On the surface this challenges the compassionate tendencies of many therapists!]

With respect to concerns about dependency and transference we find (p. 61):

The extensive use of confronting and provoking techniques throughout therapy is designed to lessen the chances of dependent relationships which seem to plague other forms of therapy. And finally the provocative therapist does not believe in silences (Jonathan Winters type monologues are preferable) and usually the stimuli presented will cause the client to respond overtly.

Here are a few separate gems:

Many therapists prefer to eternally hint to the client rather than tell him bluntly and quickly. (p. 62) [Milton Erickson was a master of direct and blunt statements from time to time.]

The client has the right to the therapist's reactions and ideas about him and to feedback from other sources that the therapist might know about. What the client's "best friends" won't tell, the therapist must provide, i.e. accurate, immediate feedback, both positive and negative. We have found that genuine rejection (of certain behaviors) is definitely more therapeutic than phony acceptance or a non-engaged indifference. (pp. 62–63) [The honesty of the therapist is therapeutic.]

In most responses the provocative therapist does everything in "larger than life" style. Voice intensity is louder than normal conversation, and everything is amplified. There is a strong element of drama and hyperbole throughout therapy. (p. 66) [It certainly helps to have had some training and experience in acting and as a comedian to be a provocative therapist!]

In effect, a constant theme of the provocative therapist is "That's nonsense. Show me. Prove it or shut up. If you have to protest it, it probably isn't true." [...] Confrontation is an important technique in provocative therapy and in many ways permeates the whole experience. (p. 70)

The therapist also communicates that he perceives much of the client's behavior as acting, i.e. under voluntary control and subject to change. (p. 72) [A client tends to say "I can't," which describes involuntary behavior. The therapist works to change that to "I won't," which is voluntary behavior.]

The why questions that clients ask very often are simply lampooned. (p. 73) ["Why" questions lead nowhere.]

[With respect to contradictory messages] This communication pattern is powerful enough to drive people crazy, perhaps it can be reversed to drive people sane. (p. 78)

At this point I am going to digress by referring to a case described by Robert Lindner (1955). The case is entitled "The Jet-propelled Couch" (pp. 156–207) and is about a physicist whose work was essential to the government. This man, Kirk, spent much of his time in a science fiction type fantasy world where he traveled in space to various planets. In true psychoanalytic fashion Lindner listened to Kirk as he told his stories of life in a far off place. However, Lindner got so hooked on these tales that when Kirk had broken out of his fantasy world and wanted to tell Lindner this had occurred it took some time (actually a few sessions) before Lindner realized how involved he had become in Kirk's world! "But in these latter weeks, although discovering himself each day to be more free of the abiding delusion, Kirk, so he now told me, was still obliged to concern himself with it for the strangest of reasons. Incomprehensible though it may seem, he felt it necessary to engage in a pretense *for my sake*." That is, Kirk did not want to "hurt" Lindner by telling him that his delusion was over!

The strange conclusion that I draw from "The Jet-propelled Couch" is that **in any two-person interaction only one person can be crazy at a time**. In a sense, provocative therapy is an application of this idea. From the client's viewpoint the provocative therapist appears to be crazier than she is in terms of the "normal" behavior of therapists. This craziness on the part of the therapist then drives the client out of her craziness! This is undoubtedly a fantastical observation. Let's return to Farrelly and Brandsma's book...

With respect to ridicule they write (p. 102), "Ridicule is the form of humor which raises the most professional eyebrows and questions, and perhaps rightfully so, for if it is not qualified, it can be hurtful. [...] Again it needs to be stressed that the provocative therapist ridicules not only the *client's* ideas and behaviors, but also his own role and "professional dignity."

Here are three more quotes:

> We want the client to vigorously and insistently protest against his own self-destructive attitudes which have been externalized by the therapist. He provokes the client with content and mock pomposity to "put him down" and be assertive with him. (p. 103)

> The therapist uses these methods to get the client to defend himself realistically against the unrealistic and excessively negative evaluation when they come from himself or others. (p. 104)

> Patients and clients do not believe in behavioral irresponsibility and neither should we. [...] We question why

many clinicians spend hours trying to convince them that "I, unlike the rest of society, can accept you and like you no matter how you behave." (p. 106)

On page 131 the authors summarize that the provocative therapist attempts to provoke the client to engage in five types of behavior:

1. To affirm his own worth both verbally and behaviorally
2. To assert himself appropriately
3. To defend himself realistically
4. To learn necessary discriminations to respond appropriately
5. To engage in risk-taking in relationships

On pages 145–157 the authors describe ways of using provocative therapy in groups.

29.2 Some Concluding Comments

I hope that you have been as fascinated by provocative therapy as I have been (and still am). This approach is not for everyone and certainly requires some training and experience before attempting to use it with difficult clients (the only kind that tempts me to be provocative). It might seem to be a treatment of last resort, although it was never this in Farrelly's hands.

Provocative therapy may be "old," yet its use should be seriously considered with the caveat of caution if you are inexperienced.

Part III

When All Else Fails, What's Next?

Chapter Thirty

So, What's Next?

30.1 Introduction to Part III

This book is obviously quite personal with respect to the topics covered and the way that they were presented. The initial motivation for writing the book came from the workshops I do where most of the attendees are relatively young (compared to me!) and appear to have been trained or taught in their programs about a limited number of ways of doing therapy and counseling. Some of the older methods in which I had been trained and which I studied were apparently unknown to them. This book is then my way of remedying this situation by discussing the oldies, but goodies, as well as some recent developments. In Part I it was also a way of emphasizing aspects of doing therapy that I feel are sometimes overlooked.

I was feeling good about being a messiah for all of these wonderful ways of doing therapy, until some colleagues of mine recommended that I read a book by authors I had never even heard of. The book was *Their Finest Hour* by Jeffrey Kottler and Jon Carlson (2011). I bought and read the book. To my astonishment, and a serious blow to my ego, I discovered that Kottler and Carlson had been in the therapy business for a long time, were quite well known, and had written many books (together and separately) along with oodles of research papers. How had *I* missed them and their contributions? To further compound my misery at this discovery I found that I was not familiar with the names or work of most of the "master therapists" who contributed chapters to their book!

In addition to this, my friend and colleague Michael F. Hoyt invited me to submit a chapter to a book he was editing entitled *Therapist Stories of Inspiration, Passion, and Renewal. What's Love Got To Do With It?* (Hoyt, 2013). I did so and it was accepted, but of the twenty-seven other contributors I only knew the work of about half, and for some of them only a small amount. I was once again confronted with the limits of my experience and knowledge of the field! This was quite humbling, to say the least. Nevertheless, here we are at the end of this book.

In the world of psychotherapy there are over 500 named (and acronymed) methods of doing therapy. It is no wonder then that all of us practitioners in the field are woefully remiss and ignorant. I continue to buy and read new books in the field, and attend workshops and conferences; I also periodically review books and recordings for the Milton H. Erickson Foundation Newsletter, which keeps me moderately current. However, all I can plead to at this moment is that in my limited experience I consider the material in this book to be practical and useful, and a highly personal statement.

Before closing this section let me emphasize the work of Scott D. Miller and Barry L. Duncan on the importance of doing beginning and end of session assessments, no matter what your orientation. You can freely download these assessments from their websites: <www.talkingcure.com>

30.2 So, What's Next?

In this concluding section I want to write a bit about a remarkable man who contributed much to our understanding of the modern world, and one of his observations—the technological imperative—which has influenced my life.

First a brief biography taken from Wikipedia: "Lewis Mumford (October 19, 1895–January 26, 1990) was an American historian, sociologist, philosopher of technology, and influential literary critic. Particularly noted for his study of cities and urban architecture, he had a broad career as a writer."

Mumford analyzed the effects of technology and urbanization on human societies, criticizing the dehumanizing tendencies of modern technological society and urging that it be brought into harmony with humanistic goals and aspirations. The following quote is about this influence:

> Western society has accepted as unquestionable a tech-
> nological imperative that is quite as arbitrary as the most
> primitive taboo: not merely the duty to foster invention
> and constantly to create technological novelties, but
> equally the duty to surrender to these novelties uncondi-
> tionally, just because they are offered, without respect to
> their human consequences.

Mumford stated that the *technological imperative* came into full
force as a driver in Western civilization during the Industrial Revolution in the nineteenth century. Effectively, what it states is that *if*
it is possible to build something bigger, stronger, faster, and more
complex, then this has to be done. Think for a moment of the yearly
increase in speed and capacity and decrease in the size of comput-
ers. My first laboratory computer had 16KB of RAM, and the laptop
we recently purchased has 8GB of RAM! Because it was possible to
go to the moon, this had to be done. Because it is possible to manipulate economies to make more profit, this has to be done. Etcetera,
etcetera, etcetera.

The technological imperative has a corollary in our personal
lives. Because it is possible to do this, that, or the other does not
mean that we have to do it. I am a fairly competent person in many
areas and receive requests from time to time to do various volunteer or paid activities. Just because I know I can do those things,
and perhaps better than some others, it does not mean I *have* to do
them. This was a great discovery to me at one time in my life. We
do have choice, and even if it is possible to do something or buy
something that does not mean we have to do it. Western civilization (followed closely by other countries) appears to be stuck in the
technological imperative. What needs to be primary to our way of
thinking is based on finding out for ourselves what is *really really
really* important in our lives, and then acting on that.

I hope that you have learned a few useful things in this book
from my wanderings over the field of psychotherapy and my experiences in the field. I find people to be endlessly interesting. I am
also enamored of learning new ways to do things as well as appreciating in different ways what I have learned in the past. Life is full
of choices for change, and if you are not changing, you are most
probably dead in some way. I like the advice I was given once that
"You have to give the Old Guy with the Scythe a moving target." I
recall when I turned forty that I was quite sad and depressed about

being so old, since it meant that there were so many books I would not be able to read, so many places I would not be able to go, so many things I would not be able to do. Now that I am in my ninth decade of life…

Thank you.

References

Andreas, A. (2012*). Transforming Negative Self-Talk: Practical, Effective Exercises.* New York: W.W. Norton and Company.

Bandler, R., and Grinder, J. (1975). *The Structure of Magic: A Book about Language and Therapy.* Palo Alto, CA: Science and Behavior Books, Inc.

Bandler, R., and Grinder, J. (1975). *Patterns of the Hypnotic Techniques of Milton H. Erickson, M.D.* Vol 1. Cupertino, CA: Meta Publications.

Bank, W. O. (1985). "Hypnotic suggestion for the control of bleeding in the angiography suite." In S. R. Lankton (Ed.), *Ericksonian Monographs No. 1: Elements and Dimensions of an Ericksonian Approach.* (pp. 76–88). New York: Brunner/Mazel.

Battino, R. (1973). "If it isn't FUN, what is it?" *ERM Journal, 5,* 107.

Battino, R. (2000). *Guided Imagery and Other Approaches to Healing.* Carmarthen, UK: Crown House Publishing Limited.

Battino, R. (2002). *Metaphoria: Metaphor and Guided Metaphor for Psychotherapy and Healing.* Carmarthen, UK: Crown House Publishing Limited.

Battino, R. (2002). *Meaning: A Play Based on the Life of Viktor E. Frankl.* Carmarthen, UK: Crown House Publishing Limited.

Battino, R. (2006). *Expectation: The Very Brief Therapy Book.* Carmarthen, UK: Crown House Publishing Limited.

Battino, R. (2008). *That's Right, is it Not? A Play about the Life of Milton H. Erickson, M.D.* Phoenix: The Milton H. Erickson Foundation Press.

Battino, R. (2011). *Healing Language: A Guide for Physicians, Dentists, Nurses, Psychologists, Social Workers, and Counselors.* <www.lulu.com>

Battino, R., and South, T. L. (2005). *Ericksonian Approaches: A Comprehensive Manual.* Carmarthen, UK: Crown House Publishing Limited.

Beaulieu, D. (2003). *Eye Movement Integration Therapy: The Comprehensive Clinical Guide.* Carmarthen, UK: Crown House Publishing Limited.

Beck, J. S., and Beck, A. T. (2011). *Cognitive Behavior Therapy (2nd Ed.): Basics and Beyond.* New York: The Guilford Press.

Berg, I. K., and Dolan, Y. (2001). *Tales of Solutions: A Collection of Hope-inspiring Stories.* New York: W.W. Norton and Company.

Bodenhamer, B. G., and Hall, L. M. (2000). *The User's Manual for the Brain. Vol. 1: The Complete Manual for Neuro-linguistic Programming Practitioner Certification.* Carmarthen, UK: Crown House Publishing Limited.

Burns, G. W. (1998). *Nature Guided Therapy. Brief Integrating Strategies for Health and Well-being.* New York: Brunner/Mazel (Taylor and Francis).

Byock, I. (2004). *The Four Things that Matter Most: A Book about Living.* New York: Free Press (Simon & Schuster).

Byock, I. (1997). *Dying Well: The Prospect for Growth at the End of Life.* New York: Riverhead Books.

Cheek, D. B. (1959). "Unconscious perception of meaningful sounds during surgical anesthesia as revealed under hypnosis." *American Journal of Clinical Hypnosis, 1*, pp. 101–113.

Cheek, D. B. (1960a). "Use of preoperative hypnosis to protect patients from careless conversation." *American Journal of Clinical Hypnosis, 3*(2), pp. 101–102.

Cheek, D. B. (1960b). "What does the surgically anesthetized patient hear?" *Rocky Mountain Medical Journal, 57*, pp. 49–53.

Cheek, D. B. (1961). "Unconscious reactions and surgical risk." *Western Journal of Surgery, Obstetrics, and Gynecology, 69*, pp. 325–328.

Cheek, D. B. (1964). "Further evidence of persistence of hearing under chemanesthesia: detailed case report." *American Journal of Clinical Hypnosis, 7*(1), pp. 55–59.

Cheek, D. B. (1965). "Can surgical patients react to what they hear under anesthesia?" *Journal American Association Nurse Anesthetists, 33*, pp. 30–38.

Cheek, D. B. (1966). "The meaning of continued hearing sense under general anesthesia." *American Journal of Clinical Hypnosis, 8*, pp. 275–280.

Cheek, D. B. (1981). "Awareness of meaningful sounds under general anesthesia: considerations and a review of the literature." In H. J. Wain's *Theoretical and Clinical Aspects of Hypnosis.* Miami: Symposia Specialists Inc.

Cheek, D. B., and LeCron , L. (1968). *Clinical Hypnotherapy.* New York: Grune and Stratton.

Cheek, D. B. (1994). *Hypnosis: The application of ideomotor techniques.* Needham Heights, MA: Allyn and Bacon.

Chevreul, M. E. (1833). "Lettre M. Ampere, sur une classe particuliere de mouvemens musculaires." *Revue des Deux Mondes, 2*, 2nd Ed., pp. 249–257.

Clawson, T. A., and Swade, R. H. (1975). "The hypnotic control of blood flow and pain: the cure of warts and the potential for the use of hypnosis in the treatment of cancer." *American Journal of Clinical Hypnosis, 17*, 160–169.

Dayton, T., and Moreno Z. (2005). *The Living Stage: A Step-by-step Guide to Psychodrama, Sociometry and Group Psychotherapy.* Dearfield Beach, FL: Health Communications Inc.

Dubin, L. L., and Shapiro, S. S. (1974). "Use of hypnosis to facilitate dental extraction and homeostasis in a classic hemophiliac with a high antibody titer to factor VIII." *American Journal of Clinical Hypnosis, 17*, pp. 79–83.

Esterling, B. A., L'Abate, L., Murray, E., and Pennebaker, J. M. (1999). "Empirical foundations for writing in prevention and psychotherapy: Mental and physical outcomes." *Clinical Psychology Review, 19*, pp. 79–96.

Ewin, M. E., and Eimer, B. N. (2006). *Ideomotor Signals for Rapid Hypnoanalysis: A How-to Manual.* Springfield, IL: Charles C. Thomas Publisher, Ltd.

Farrelly, F., and Brandsma, J. (1974). *Provocative Therapy.* San Francisco: Celestial Arts (Shields Publishing Co., Inc.)

Fink, H. H., and Battino, R. (2011). *Howie and Ruby: Conversations 2000–2007.* <www.lulu.com>

Frankl, V. E. (1984). *Man's Search for Meaning: An Introduction to Logotherapy.* New York: Simon & Schuster (A Touchstone Book).

Freedman, J., and Combs, G. (1996). *Narrative Therapy: The Social Construction of Preferred Results.* New York: W.W. Norton & Company.

Hall, L. M., and Bodenhamer, B. G. (2003). *The User's Manual for the Brain. Vol. II: Mastering Systemic NLP.* Carmarthen, UK: Crown House Publishing Limited.

Grinder, J., and Bandler, R. (1976). *The Structure of Magic II: A Book about Communication and Change.* Palo Alto, CA: Science and behavior Books, Inc.

Grinder, J., DeLozier, J., and Bandler, R. (1977). *Patterns of the Hypnotic Techniques of Milton H. Erickson, M.D.* Vol. 2. Cupertino, CA: Meta Publications.

Holmes, P., Karp, M., and Watson, M. (1994). *Psychodrama Since Moreno: Innovations in Theory and Practice.* New York: Taylor & Francis (Routledge).

Hoyt, M. F. (2013). *Therapist Stories of Inspiration, Passion and Renewal: What's Love Got To Do With It?* New York: Routledge (Taylor & Francis Group).

Hubble, M. A., Duncan, B. L., and Miller, S. D. (1999). *The Heart and Soul of Change: What Works in Therapy.* Washington, D.C.: American Psychological Association.

James, T., and Woodsmall, W. (1988). *Time Line Therapy and the Basis of Personality.* Cupertino, CA: Meta Publications.

Kacewicz, E., Slatcher, R. B., and Pennebaker, J. W. "Expressive writing: An alternative to traditional methods." In L. L'Abate's (Ed.), *Low-cost Approaches to Promote Physical and Mental Health: Theory, Research, and Practice.* New York: Springer.

Karp, M., Holmes, P., and Tauvon, K. B. (1998). *The Handbook of Psychodrama.* New York: Taylor & Francis (Routledge).

Keeney, H. and Keeney, B. (2012). *Circular Therapeutics: Giving Therapy a Healing Heart.* Phoenix: Zeig, Tucker & Theisen.

Koerner, K., and Linehan, M. M. (2012). *Dialectical Behavior Therapy: A Practical Guide.* New York: The Guilford Press.

Kottler, J., and Carlson, J. (2011). *Their Finest Hour: Master Therapists Share Their Greatest Success Stories.* Carmarthen, UK: Crown House Publishing Limited.

L'Abate, L. (1991). "The use of writing in psychotherapy." *American Journal of Psychotherapy, 45,* pp. 87–98.

L'Abate, L. (1992). *Programmed Writing: A Self-administered Approach for Interventions with Individuals, Couples and Families.* Pacific Grove, CA: Brooks/ Cole.

L'Abate, L. (1997). "Distance-writing and computer-assisted training." In S. R. Saber's (Ed.), *Managed Mental Health Care: Major Diagnostic and Treatment Approaches*, pp. 133–163, Bristol, PA: Brunner/Mazel.

L'Abate, L. (2007). *Low-cost Approaches to Promote Physical and Mental Health: Theory, Research, and Practice.* (Ed.). New York: Springer.

L'Abate, L. (2011). *Sourcebook of Interactive Practice Exercises in Mental Health.* New York: Springer.

LeShan, L. (1974). *How to Meditate: A Guide to Self-discovery.* New York: Bantam Books.

LeShan, L. (1977). *You Can Fight for your Life.* New York: M. Evans & Co., Inc.

Leshan, L. (1982). *The Mechanic and the Gardener.* New York: Holt, Rinehart & Winston.

LeShan, L. (1989). *Cancer as a Turning Point.* New York: A Plume Book (Penguin Books).

LeShan, L. (2012). *Landscapes of the Mind: The Faces of Reality.* Guilford, CT: Eirini Press.

Lindner, R. (1955). *The Fifty-minute Hour: A Collection of True Psychoanalytic tales.* New York: Bantam Books.

Linehan, M. M. (1993). *Cognitive-behavioral Treatment of Borderline Personality Disorder.* New York: The Guilford Press.

Liu, W. H. D., Standen, P. J., and Aitkenhead, A. R. (1992). "Therapeutic suggestions during general anesthesia in patients undergoing hysterectomy." *British Journal of Anesthesia, 68,* pp. 277–281.

Lowen, A. (1958). *The Language of the Body.* New York: Grune and Stratton (Macmillan Publishing Company).

Lowen, A. (1975). *Bioenergetics.* New York: Coward, McCann & Geoghegan, Inc.

Mann, D. (2010). *Gestalt Therapy: 100 Key Points and Techniques.* New York: Routledge (Taylor & Francis Group).

Maxfield, L., Shapiro, F., and Kaslow, F. W. (2007). *Handbook of EMDR and Family Therapy Processes.* New York: Wiley & Sons.

Miller, S. D., and Berg, I. K. (1995). *The Miracle Method: A Radically New Approach to Problem Drinking.* New York: W.W. Norton & Company.

Miller, S. D., Hubble, M. A., and Duncan, B. L. (Eds.), (1996). *Handbook of Solution-focused Brief Therapy.* San Francisco: Jossey-Bass Publishers.

Moreno, J. L. (1972). *Psychodrama.* Beacon, NY: Beacon House Inc.

Nardone, G., and Portelli, C. (2005). *Knowing Through Changing: The Evolution of Brief Strategic Therapy.* Carmarthen, UK: Crown House Publishing Ltd.

O'Hanlon, W. H. (1994). "The third wave" *Family Therapy Networker,* pp. 19–29.

O'Hanlon, B. (2003). *A Guide to Inclusive Therapy: 26 Methods of Respectful Resistance-dissolving Therapy.* New York: W.W. Norton and Company.

Pearson, R. E. (1961). "Response to suggestions given under general anesthesia." *American Journal of Clinical Hypnosis, 4,* pp. 106–114.

Pennebaker, J. W. (1997). "Writing about emotional experiences as a therapeutic process." *Psychological Science, 8,* pp. 162–166.

Pennebaker, J. W., and Chung, C. K. (2007). "Expressive writing, emotional upheavals, and health." In H. Friedman and B. Silver (Eds.), *Handbook of Health Psychology*, pp. 263–284. New York: Oxford University Press.

Perls, F. S. (1969). *Gestalt Therapy Verbatim*. Moab, UT: Real People Press (reprinted by Bantam Books).

Polster, E., and Polster, M. (1974). *Gestalt Therapy Integrated: Contours of Theory and Practice*. New York: Vintage Books.

Polster, E. (1987). *Every Person's Life is Worth a Novel*. New York: W.W. Norton & Company.

Remen, R. N. (1996). *Kitchen Table Wisdom: Stories that Heal*. New York: Riverhead Books

Rossi, E. L., and Cheek, D. B. (1988). *Mind–body Therapy: Ideodynamic Healing in Hypnosis*. New York: W.W. Norton & Co.

Schutz, W. C. (1989). *Joy: Twenty Years Later: Expanding Human Awareness*. Berkeley, CA: Ten Speed Press.

Seligman, M. E. P. (2003). *Authentic Happiness: Using the New Positive Psychology to Realize your Potential for Lasting Fulfillment*. New York: The Free Press (Simon & Schuster, Inc).

Shapiro, A. K., and Shapiro, E. (1997). *The Powerful Placebo: From Ancient Priest to Modern Physician*. Baltimore: The Johns Hopkins University Press.

Shapiro, F. (2001). *Eye Movement Desensitization and Reprocessing: Basic Principles, Protocols, and Procedures* (2nd ed.). New York: Guildford Press.

de Shazer, S. (1985). *Keys to Solution in Brief Therapy*. New York: W.W. Norton & Company.

de Shaver, S. (1988). *Clues: Investigating Solutions in Brief Therapy*. W.W. Norton & Company.

de Shazer, S. (1991). *Putting Difference to Work*. New York: W.W. Norton & Company.

de Shazer, S. (1994). *Words were Originally Magic*. New York: W.W. Norton & Company.

Siegel, B. S. (1990). *Love, Medicine and Miracles: Lessons Learned about Self-healing from a Surgeon's Experience with Exceptional Patients*. New York: HarperCollins.

Silvester, T. (2003). *Wordweaving: The Science of Suggestion—a comprehensive guide to creating hypnotic language*. Berks, England: Berkley House.

Silvester, T. (2006). *Wordweaving Vol II: The Question is the Answer*. Burwell, Cambs, UK: The Quest Institute.

Silvester, T. (2010). *Cognitive Hypnotherapy: "What's that about and how can I use it?"* Leicester, UK: Matador. (www.troubador.co.uk/matador)

Snyder, E. D. (1971). *Hypnotic Poetry: A Study of Trance-inducing Technique in Certain Poems and its Literary Significance*. New York: Octagon Books.

Stevens, J. O. (Andreas, Steve) (2008). *Awareness: Exploring, Experimenting, Experiencing*. Gouldsboro, ME: The Gestalt Journal Press.

Talmon, M. (1990). *Single-session Therapy: Maximizing the Effect of the First (and often only) Therapeutic Encounter*. San Francisco: Jossey-Bass Publishers.

Wampold, B. E. (2001). *The Great Psychotherapy Debate: Models, Methods, and Findings*. Mahway, NJ: Lawrence Erlbaum Associates, Publishers.

Watzlawick, P.; Weakland, J. Ch. E.; and Fisch, R. (1974). *Change: Principles of Problem Formation and Problem Resolution*. New York: W.W. Norton & Company.

Weiner-Davis, M.; de Shazer, S.; and Gingerich, W. J., (1987). "Building pre-treatment change to construct the therapeutic solution: An exploratory study." *Journal of Marital and Family Therapy, 13*, pp. 359–363.

White, M. (2007). *Maps of Narrative Practice*. New York: W.W. Norton & Company.

White, M., and Epston, D. (1990). *Narrative Means to Therapeutic Ends*. New York: W.W. Norton & Company.

Yalom, I. D., and M. Leszcz, M. (2005). *Theory and Practice of Group Psychotherapy* (5th Ed.). New York: Basic Books (Perseus Books Group).

Index